GEORGIA
Hometown Cookbook

by **Sheila Simmons** and **Kent Whitaker**

Great American Publishers
www.GreatAmericanPublishers.com

TOLL-FREE 1.888.854.5954

Great American Publishers

P. O. Box 1305 • Kosciusko, MS 39090

TOLL-FREE 1.888.854.5954 • www.GreatAmericanPublishers.com

ISBN 978-1-934817-01-8 (1-934817-01-5)

Printed in Canada

FIRST EDITION
10 9 8 7 6 5 4 3 2 1

by Sheila Simmons & Kent Whitaker

Designed by Roger & Sheila Simmons

Front cover photos: Midtown Atlanta Skyline: Thomas Nord shutterstock.com • Cherokee Rose: Ron Blanton shutter-stock.com • Tybee Light: Cindy Haggerty bigstockphoto.com • Food: © Food Image Source, John Kelly, StockFood, Pecan Meringue Peach Pie p227

Back cover photos: Apple Bars: Ewa Kubicka bigstockphoto.com • Yumion: ©Vidalia Area Convention & Visitors Bureau

Inside photos: istockphoto.com: Half Title p1 © Cynthia Baldauf • Appetizers p9 © Dragan Trifunovic • Bread & Breakfast p29 © Thomas Perkins • Salads p51 © Kelly Cline • Soups, Stews, Chili, & Chowders p67 © Thomas Perkins • Vegetables & Other Side Dishes p83 © Diane Diederich • Pork p97 © Karin Lau • Beef p117 © Carol Gering • Fish & Seafood p159 © Suzanne Tucker • Cookies & Candies p179 © Jim Jurica • Cakes p199 © Jim Jurica • shutterstock.com: Pies & Other Desserts p219 © giordano borghi • Index p241 © Anita Patterson Peppers • bigstockphoto.com: Poultry p137 © Paul Clarke

Georgia

Contents

Hometown Cookbook

6 ·

Introduction

When my cookbook partner, Kent Whitaker, and I decided to start the Hometown Cookbook Series, we had a clear vision of what we wanted to accomplish... a state-by-state cookbook series that will preserve those recipes that have been handed down through generations. You know the recipes... the ones your children always want you to make on their birthday, the dish you take to the church supper then spend the rest of the afternoon giving out the recipe for because everyone liked it so much, that recipe your grandmother then your mother then you have made for so many years no one remembers where it actually originated, and on and on.

As we started our year-long research of Georgia's hometown cooking, it didn't take long to discover that Georgia cooks would provide a wealth of recipes to draw upon. Indeed, great cooks abound in the Peach Tree State. As expected, many of the recipes feature the products found so readily in the state... peaches, Vidalia onions, peanuts, pecans, and much more. Delicious recipes like *Millionaire Peach Salad*, *Pecan Meringue Peach Pie*, *Georgia Goober Butter Cookies*, and *Easy Peach Crisp*.

From fast-paced city life in Atlanta, to the quiet glory of the North Georgia mountains, to fun in the sun on the Atlantic coast, to the small towns, woodlands, and rivers found all over the state, Southern hospitality is abundant in Georgia where there is something for everyone to enjoy. From traditional favorites like *Georgia Deviled Eggs*, *Fried Corn*, and *Stewed Cabbage and Beef*... to new and diverse recipes like *Georgia Peach Pasta Salad*, *Strawberry Kisses*, and *Jalapeño Shrimp Pops*... to *Georgia's Favorite Brunswick Stew*... There is definitely something for everyone to enjoy, too, when it comes to Georgia's hometown cooking.

Nowhere is Georgia's Southern hospitality more evident than during the many festivals that are held throughout the state each year. And throughout this book, you'll enjoy fun stories and pictures about food-related festivals across the state. From the Georgia Apple Festival in Ellijay to the Jekyll Island Shrimp & Grits Festival from Taste of Atlanta to Colquitt's National Mayhaw Festival, there's a celebration to suit every taste.

Our gratitude goes to the many gracious people associated with these festivals. You were helpful and generous with your time and this book is all the better for the assistance you provided. Our sincerest appreciation is also extended to Leigh Prestage, research assistant extraordinaire, and Anita Musgrove and Wendy Musgrove, the best hometown salespeople around. As always a big thank you goes to our families for their unwavering support; Ally and Macee, Roger, Ryan, and Nicholas—we couldn't do it without you.

We sincerely hope you enjoy using this latest edition of our Hometown Cookbook Series as much as we enjoyed writing it. When it comes to Georgia hometown cooking, there's a lot to love and this book brings you the very best the Peach Tree State has to offer.

Wishing you many happy kitchen memories,

Sheila Simmons & Kent Whitaker

Appetizers

Sweet Georgia Brown Orange Tea

5 tea bags
4 cups boiling water
1 can frozen orange juice concentrate, thawed
1 can frozen lemon juice concentrate, thawed
10 cups water
⅔ cup sugar
Sliced lemons

Allow tea bags to steep in boiling water 5 minutes; discard tea bags. In a large pot or sturdy tea pitcher combine steeped tea, orange juice, lemon juice, water and sugar. Stir until dissolved. Serve chilled over ice with a lemon wedge.

Georgia Peach Smoothie

1 (16-ounce) can peaches
1 banana
1 (1-serving cup) vanilla yogurt
French vanilla coffee creamer to taste
4 cups ice

Combine in a blender and mix until smooth. Serve in a glass. Add water or milk if needed.

Nobody makes a smoothie like my wife Ally who was born in Columbus, Georgia. Her secret ingredient is a few drips of French vanilla coffee creamer.

Frozen Fruit Blast

2 cups grape juice
2 cups orange juice
1 (2-liter) bottle lemon-lime soda
Crushed ice
Vanilla ice cream

Combine all ingredients in a blender. Blend until smooth.
Serve with flavored rum, if desired. Thin with milk if needed.

Georgia Coastal Rum Runner

8 to 10 shots pineapple rum
1 (2-liter) bottle orange-flavored drink
1 can crushed pineapple
Crushed ice

Combine rum, orange drink and pineapple. Mix well and serve over crushed ice.

Scott Hunsucker

Cordele-Crisp County Melon Punch

1 cup sugar
¼ cup water
2 (2-inch) sticks cinnamon
6 cups grapefruit juice
3 cups orange juice
1 quart watermelon juice

Heat sugar and water for 10 minutes. Add remaining ingredients and chill.

Watermelon Days Festival

Watermelon Days Festival
Cordele • June

Come discover the magic of Cordele Crisp County at the annual Watermelon Days Festival. Each summer, we celebrate the harvest of the crop that has made us famous. Our festival is the oldest in the state and offers a variety of activities during June. Events include a Watermelon Queen Pageant, Watermelon Dance, Talent Show, Gospel Sing, Decorating, Eating, Chunking, Seed Spit Contests, and a Watermelon Walk. There are activities for children, including a Parade, Fishing Rodeo, Puppet and Dog Show. There's something for everyone!

229.273.1668
www.cordele-crisp-chamber.com

Craig Leaper · www.bigstockphoto.com

Georgia

Cordele-Crisp County Watermelon Cocktail

1 large watermelon
Ginger ale (or pink champagne)

Using a melon baller, remove all meat from watermelon. Soak watermelon balls in ginger ale several hours in refrigerator before serving. Serve in chilled cocktail glasses.

Watermelon Days Festival

KJ's Touchdown Taco Dip

1 pound ground beef
1 tablespoon Mrs. Dash seasoning
1 tablespoon crushed red pepper
1 tablespoon minced garlic
1 (16-ounce) carton sour cream
1 (8-ounce) package cream cheese, softened
1 package taco seasoning
1 can refried beans
2 cups shredded mixed cheese
½ cup halved black olives
½ cup diced tomatoes
½ cup chopped onion
½ cup chopped jalapeño peppers, optional

Brown ground beef with Mrs. Dash seasoning, crushed red pepper and minced garlic; drain. Combine sour cream, cream cheese and taco seasoning in a bowl. In a large glass baking dish sprayed with nonstick spray, spread refried beans across bottom. Spread meat evenly over beans. Spread sour cream mixture over meat; bake at 450° until edges brown. Spread cheese over top and return to oven until cheese is melted. Top with remaining ingredients and serve hot with chips.

Jamie Campbell • Ringgold, Georgia

Georgia Bulldog Deep Dish Tailgate Dip

1 (8-ounce) package cream cheese, softened
1 (16-ounce) carton sour cream
½ tablespoon minced garlic
Salt and pepper to taste
1 can or jar pizza sauce
½ pound ground sausage, browned
2 cups shredded cheese (mozzarella or your choice)

Combine cream cheese, sour cream, garlic, salt and pepper. Spread in bottom of large foil pan. Cover with pizza sauce, sausage and cheese. Bake about 30 minutes at 350°. Serve during your tailgate party with chips for dipping.

Ramblin' Wreck Tech Dip

1 can whole-kernel corn, drained
1 can black beans, drained and rinsed
1 can diced tomatoes, drained
1 green bell pepper, diced
1 small onion, chopped
½ tablespoon cilantro
½ tablespoon Italian seasoning
Garlic powder to taste
Black pepper to taste
1 tablespoon hot sauce

Mix everything together; chill before serving. Serve with chips or crackers.

Hot Corn Scoopin' Dip

1 can whole-kernel corn, drained
1 can diced tomatoes & chilies, drained
1 (8-ounce) package cream cheese, diced and softened
½ teaspoon chili powder
½ teaspoon garlic powder
Chopped fresh cilantro to taste

Combine everything in a baking dish. Bake at 350° about 20 minutes. Stir and serve warm with chips, veggies or crackers.

Variation: Leave out the cream cheese and add a few squirts of lemon juice. Mix well, chill and serve with crackers.

Easy Vidalia Onion Chili Queso Dip

1 jar pasteurized process cheese spread
⅓ cup milk
½ cup chopped Vidalia onions
1 can hot dog chili
1 small can chopped green chilies

Heat all ingredients on low heat, stirring constantly, about 2 minutes or until cheese is melted. Pour into fondue pot or chafing dish; keep warm over low heat. Serve with corn chips, tortilla chips or raw vegetables.

Vidalia Onion Spicy Ranch Dip

1 (16-ounce) container sour cream
1 package ranch seasoning
1 tablespoon mayonnaise
2 tablespoons Dijon mustard
2 tablespoons minced vidalia onion

Combine all ingredients, cover and chill before serving.

Simple Tarragon-Chive Dip

⅔ cup mayonnaise
⅓ cup chopped tarragon leaves
1⅓ cups sour cream
3 tablespoons finely chopped fresh chives
½ teaspoon garlic powder
1½ teaspoons lime juice
Salt and pepper to taste
¼ cup milk, optional

This is a tasty dip that can be made in just a few minutes.

Combine all ingredients; use milk for a thinner dip or leave it out for a thicker dip. Cover, chill and serve.

Quick 'n Easy Homemade French Onion Dip

1 (8-ounce) package cream cheese, softened
½ cup sour cream
1 envelope onion soup mix
1 tablespoon Worcestershire sauce
1½ teaspoons garlic salt
Dash of milk or water

Combine all ingredients in a mixing bowl; mix well using an electric mixer. Add a splash of water or milk if you feel the dip is too thick. For a smooth dip, strain onion soup mix through a sifter. For even more onion flavor, add a tablespoon of chopped Vidalia onions.

Providence Canyon State Park
Lumpkin

Peach Guacamole

5 medium avocados, peeled and finely chopped
1 cup chopped fresh cilantro
Salt, black pepper, garlic salt and cayenne pepper
1 medium Georgia peach, peeled and finely chopped
Juice of 1 lime

A traditional Mexican favorite with a Georgia twist.

Process ⅔ chopped avocado in a food processor until smooth. Add seasonings to taste; process until well mixed. In a large glass bowl, combine processed avocado with remaining avocado, peaches, and lime juice; stir gently until fully mixed. Chill before serving with chips for dipping.

Avocado Dip

1 avocado, mashed
1 small tomato, chopped
½ small onion, chopped
½ tablespoon crushed red pepper
½ tablespoon lemon or lime juice
Large dash salt and pepper

Mix well and chill before serving.

Georgia-Pecan Party-Time Zesty Cheese Ball

3 (8-ounce) packages cream cheese, softened
½ cup crumbled blue cheese
½ pound shredded Cheddar cheese
½ pound shredded Pepper Jack cheese
3 tablespoons soy sauce
1 teaspoon ground pepper
½ tablespoon minced garlic
2 tablespoons minced onion
½ tablespoon minced jalapeño, if desired
Chopped Georgia pecans

Blend all ingredients except pecans. Form into 1 large ball or 2 small ones and roll firmly in chopped pecans.

Vidalia Onion Farm Fresh Salsa

1 pound tomatoes, diced
½ large Vidalia onion, finely chopped
1 tablespoon minced garlic
¼ cup chopped parsley
1 tablespoon lime juice
½ teaspoon ground coriander
½ teaspoon salt
½ teaspoon black pepper

Vidalia onions and fresh tomatoes make this a very tasty, but not hot, salsa. Ally and I make this salsa every summer using farm-fresh tomatoes grown by our buddy, Mr. Bowan, in North Georgia.

Combine everything in a covered bowl. Chill at least an hour before serving.

Red Hot Vidalia Onion Salsa

1 pound tomatoes, diced
1 Vidalia onion, chopped
1 green bell pepper, chopped
½ tablespoon minced garlic
2 jalapeño peppers, chopped
1 tablespoon chopped cilantro
1½ tablespoons lemon or lime juice
3 tablespoons hot sauce
1 teaspoon black pepper
2 teaspoons cumin powder

Combine everything in a covered bowl. Chill at least an hour before serving.

Mango Creamy Salsa

2 cups finely chopped mango
½ cup finely chopped red bell pepper
½ cup finely chopped red onion
1 tablespoon chopped cilantro
1 jalapeño pepper, chopped
1 tablespoon lemon or lime juice
Salt and Pepper to taste
1 cup sour cream

Combine all ingredients, except sour cream, cover and refrigerate at least 30 minutes to blend flavors. Before serving, stir in sour cream and mix well. Serve chilled.

Lea Hunsucker, a teacher in Northern Georgia who enjoys visiting family on St. Simons Island

Fireside Bacon Spread

1 (8-ounce) package cream cheese, softened
½ cup mayonnaise
1 to 2 tablespoons minced dried onion
6 ounces shredded Swiss cheese
1 cup real bacon bits

Combine all ingredients and chill. Spread over finger-sized slices of toast, melba toast or crackers.

Macee Whitaker

Pickle & Ham Pin Wheels

1 tub cream cheese
1 package tortilla spinach wraps
⅔ (1-pound) package sliced ham
1 small jar sweet pickles, chopped
1 bag spinach leaves, rinsed and dried
Salt and pepper

I like using flavored cream cheese for this recipe. You can also substitute pimento cheese if you wish.

Spread cream cheese over wraps and top with a layer of ham then pickles. Add a layer of raw spinach leaves. Roll up tightly. Add additional cream cheese as "glue" if needed. Slice into pinwheels and secure with decorative toothpicks.

Shekkie's Spicy Jalapeño Canoes

20 to 24 jalapeño peppers
2 (8-ounce) packages cream cheese, softened
1 (8-ounce) package finely shredded Cheddar cheese, divided
1 (6- to 8-ounce) package real bacon bits

Using latex or protective gloves, cut tops off peppers; cut peppers in half, remove seeds and white membrane (all the hot stuff), and set aside on a large serving platter. In a mixing bowl, using a large fork, combine cream cheese and ¾ Cheddar; mix well. Add bacon bits (to taste) and mix well. Stuff peppers halves with mixture, level to the top of the halves. For grill: Coat or spray grill with oil, preheat to low heat, and cook peppers 10 to 12 minutes, or until cheese mixture is melted. For oven: Place pepper canoes 1 inch apart on a greased cookie sheet and cook 15 minutes at 375°. Top with remaining Cheddar cheese before serving. Serve warm.

Wes Spencer, born in Athens, Georgia

Georgia

Jalapeño Shrimp Pops

½ to ⅔ cup frozen mini (salad) shrimp
⅓ cup diced onion
2 tablespoons diced jalapeño pepper
1 (8-ounce) package cream cheese, softened
⅓ cup real bacon bits
Hot sauce to taste
2 boxes frozen mini pastry shells, thawed

Combine all ingredients, except shells, in a bowl. Mix well and spoon equal amounts of filling into shells. Bake at 375° until filling turns a light golden color.

Taste of Atlanta

Atlanta • October

Taste of Atlanta is a 2-day outdoor food festival held in the streets of Atlantic Station. The event features more than 70 of the city's best restaurants, live cooking demonstrations from national and local celebrity chefs, live entertainment and a Wine Experience. From hot new restaurants to time-tested favorites, from world cuisine to eateries that are off the beaten path, Taste of Atlanta encourages food lovers to explore the best the city has to offer.

404.875.4434 • www.tasteofatlanta.net

The food lover's food event
TASTE OF ATLANTA

Georgia Deviled Eggs

6 hard-cooked eggs, peeled
¼ teaspoon salt
¼ teaspoon pepper
1 tablespoon prepared mustard
2 tablespoons avocado, mashed
1 tablespoon sweet relish
½ teaspoon apple cider vinegar
½ tablespoon sour cream
Hot sauce (to taste)
12 green olive slices with pimentos

Cut eggs in half, lengthwise. Place yolks in 1-quart plastic bag; place whites onto a deviled egg tray. Take the bag containing yolks, press out air and mash until yolks are powdery. Add salt, pepper, mustard, avocado, sweet relish, vinegar, sour cream, and hot sauce to bag; press out air. Close bag and knead until ingredients are blended. Push filling toward corner of bag. Use scissors to snip about ½-inch off corner of bag. Squeezing bag gently, fill reserved whites with yolk mixture. Top each deviled egg with olive slices. Chill to blend flavors.

Jewell Hutto, Executive Director, Georgia Egg Commission

Georgia-Style Fancy Cucumber Sandwiches

1 package cream cheese, softened
1 tablespoon grated onion
1 tablespoon horseradish
1 tablespoon sour cream
½ cup crushed almonds
1 cucumber, peeled, grated and drained
Salt and pepper to taste
French bread loaf

Combine all ingredients, except French bread; chill. Spread evenly over horizontally sliced French bread loaf. Slice into 1¼-inch thin pieces. Cut slices in half. Hold together with a toothpick.

Sliced Cucumber Party Sandwiches

2 cucumbers, sliced
White wine vinegar
Pepper
Cream cheese, softened
Butter, softened
Party-sized bread or loaf bread (crust removed and cut in fourths)

Drizzle cucumber slices with white wine vinegar; add a dash of black pepper. Chill 30 minutes or until just before serving. Spread a small amount of cream cheese on half the bread and a small amount of butter on the other half. Drain cucumber slices and place on a paper towel to remove excess vinegar. Place a slice (or more) of cucumber between 1 cream cheese-filled slice and 1 butter-filled slice of bread. Serve immediately to keep bread from becoming mushy.

Hot Georgia Catfish Bites

½ cup all-purpose flour
¾ teaspoon baking powder
¼ teaspoon salt
⅛ teaspoon cayenne pepper
2 eggs, beaten
¼ cup milk
1 tablespoon vegetable oil
¼ teaspoon hot sauce

½ cup shredded mozzarella cheese
1 cup cooked flaked catfish
1½ cups cooked brown rice
¼ cup minced green bell pepper
¼ cup chopped jalapeño pepper
¼ cup minced onion
Oil for frying

Combine flour, baking powder, salt and cayenne pepper. Beat in eggs, milk, 1 tablespoon oil and hot sauce. Mix well; add remaining ingredients. Form into small balls. Fry in hot oil until golden brown. Serve hot with toothpicks and tartar sauce with a splash of hot sauce mixed in for dipping.

A cross between a hushpuppy and fried catfish... delicious.

Vidalia 'n Bacon Water Chestnuts

1 pound sliced bacon
3 to 4 cans whole water chestnuts
1 Vidalia onion
⅔ cup soy sauce

⅓ cup water
½ cup brown sugar
Large dash ground ginger

Cut bacon into thirds or fourths depending on size of water chestnuts. Slice onion into half from top to bottom not from side; remove skin. Cut each half in half again (or thirds depending on water chestnut size). Wrap water chestnuts in onion, then bacon and secure with a toothpick. Combine soy sauce, water, sugar and ginger in a bowl; stir until sugar is dissolved. Place wrapped chestnuts in a large, heavy-duty freezer bag; pour in marinade. Gently turn to cover all sides. Marinate about 30 minutes. Bake 15 to 20 minutes on a cookie sheet in the oven at 375°.

Cornbread Chili Cups

2 cans cornbread twists (or canned biscuits)
Corn chips
1 can chili with beans
½ cup minced onion
1 tablespoon minced jalapeño, optional
½ cup grated Monterey Jack cheese
Sour cream, as desired

Preheat oven to 350°. Divide cornbread twists into 16 sections. Roll each flat; press into bottom and sides of muffin tin. Place a small amount of corn chips in each cup then spoon equal amounts chili into each. Top with onions, and jalapeños. Cook about 15 minutes, or until bread is cooked. Top with cheese and return to oven just until cheese is melted.

Variation: If you don't like the heat of jalapeño, leave it out and try ¼ cup finely chopped bell pepper instead.

Pretzel Meat Balls

1½ pounds ground beef
1 egg, beaten
1 cup crushed pretzels
⅓ cup mustard
⅔ cup shredded cheese
Onion powder, salt and pepper

Combine everything in a large bowl. Roll into meatball-sized portions. Bake at 375° for 15 to 20 minutes. Serve hot.

Macee Whitaker

Hot Breaded Meat Balls

1 bag frozen meat balls, thawed
Hot sauce
2 cans biscuits or croissants

Cook meat balls in oven or microwave (do not overcook) or simply thaw if meat balls are precooked. Roll in hot sauce. Cut or press dough into small portions large enough to wrap completely around meat balls. Press edges together with fingers. Place on a nonstick cookie sheet and bake in oven at 350° until golden brown. Serve hot with a toothpick.

Bread & Breakfast

Cat Head Biscuits

2 cups all-purpose flour
1 tablespoon baking powder
½ tablespoon baking soda
½ teaspoon salt
⅓ cup shortening
2 tablespoons butter
⅔ cup buttermilk
Bacon grease

Some say these biscuits get as big as a cat's head. Others say the name comes from the shape of the biscuits when cooked three at a time in a cast iron skillet. All I know is they are delicious!

Combine dry ingredients. Mix in shortening and butter; stir in buttermilk. Grease a baking pan or cast iron skillet with bacon grease. Spoon dough into pan or skillet and press down a bit to flatten. Top each biscuit with a bit of bacon grease and bake 15 minutes or until golden brown.

Georgia Country-Style Pancakes

1½ cups all-purpose flour
3½ teaspoons baking powder
1 teaspoon salt
1 tablespoon sugar
3 tablespoons butter, melted
1 egg, beaten
1¼ cups milk

In a large bowl, mix all ingredients until smooth. Use a ½-cup measuring cup to form perfect-sized pancakes. Cook on a hot, greased griddle.

Molasses Drop Biscuits

2 cups self-rising flour
1 teaspoon baking powder
3 tablespoons sugar
2 teaspoons cinnamon
4 tablespoons vegetable
   shortening
2 teaspoons butter

1 egg, beaten
3 tablespoons molasses
¾ cup buttermilk
¼ cup raisins
Powdered sugar, optional
Cinnamon, optional
Molasses, optional

Preheat oven to 375°. Combine flour, baking powder, sugar and cinnamon. Using a pastry blender, cut shortening and butter into flour mixture until it looks like cornmeal. Add egg, molasses and buttermilk; mix well. Fold in raisins and drop by tablespoonfuls onto a light-colored or air-bake baking pan. Bake 10 minutes or until lightly brown. If desired, sprinkle with powdered sugar and cinnamon and spoon molasses over biscuits or serve plain.

Jewell Hutto, Executive Director, Georgia Egg Commission

Banana Pecan Pancakes

Similar to banana bread but in pancake-form; these make a very tasty breakfast.

2½ cups self-rising flour
1½ tablespoons sugar
1 tablespoon brown sugar
½ teaspoon salt
2 cups buttermilk

¼ cup vegetable oil
2 large eggs, beaten
1 cup thinly sliced bananas
½ cup chopped Georgia pecans

Combine all ingredients, except bananas and pecans, in a bowl. Mix well. Add additional milk as needed for desired thickness. Gently fold bananas and pecans into mix. Cook as you would a normal pancake. Serve hot.

North Georgia Baked Apple Breakfast

1 loaf French bread
1 can apple pie filling
5 to 6 eggs
1½ cups milk
½ cup brown sugar
1 tablespoon vanilla extract
1 jar caramel sauce, warmed in microwave
Powdered Sugar

If you have time, visit the apple orchards in the beautiful mountains of North Georgia and enjoy some fresh-baked apple pie... or, enjoy this quick-baked apple breakfast at home.

Slice French bread into 1-inch slices. In a greased 9x13-inch baking pan, layer half of the bread cutting to fit as needed. Cover with half the pie filling; repeat with remaining bread and filling. In a bowl, combine eggs, milk, sugar and vanilla in a bowl; whisk to blend. Pour over bread mixture in pan. Bake 1 hour at 350°. French toast should puff up and be firm in the center. Drizzle warmed caramel sauce over toast and sprinkle with powdered sugar.

Apple Pickin' Jubilee

Ellijay • September

The Apple Pickin' Jubilee farm festival features u-pic apples, wagon rides, petting farm, museums, live pig races, cow milking, and great food inside the market and outside in the festival area. We make our own fried apple pies, apple cider doughnuts, apple fritters, apple cider slushies, candy apples, fudge and ice cream. Join us for apple pickin' fun at the Apple Pickin' Jubilee.

706.273.3838
www.hillcrestorchards.net/jubilee.htm

image courtesy of Apple Pickin' Jubilee

Country-Style Fried Apple Pies for Breakfast

Filling

2 apples, peeled and chopped
½ teaspoon ground cinnamon
2 tablespoons apple butter
¼ cup sugar
Water

Peaches or other fruits, jelly or jams can be substituted for the apples in this versatile recipe.

Combine all and cook in a saucepan over low heat until apples are soft. Add water as needed, but not too much. Mash apples lightly to make a chunky filling.

Crust

2 cups all-purpose flour
1 teaspoon salt
½ cup shortening
½ cup water
Vegetable oil for frying
Powdered sugar

Sift flour and salt together; cut in shortening. Add water and mix with fork. Roll to about ⅛-inch thick on a floured board. Cut with a large circular cookie cutter or large-mouth plastic cup. Place a spoonful of filling in center of each circle. Fold over and pinch edges using wet finger tips to seal. Fry until golden brown. Sprinkle with powdered sugar before serving. Serve hot.

Brown Sugar Bacon

1 pound thick-sliced bacon strips
Brown sugar
Dash cinnamon

This is sometimes called sweet bacon. Try it with a hot biscuit and side of eggs. I had my first taste of sweet bacon at the NASCAR races in Atlanta.

Sprinkle brown sugar and cinnamon over bacon pieces. Lay each slice in a deep-sided baking pan; bake at 350° until crispy. Remove bacon from grease carefully and lay on a paper towel to crisp. Serve hot.

Breakfast Hash Brown Casserole

1 bag frozen hash browns, thawed
4 eggs, beaten
1 stick (½ cup) butter, melted
1 pound ground sausage, browned
1 cup shredded cheese
1 can cream of mushroom soup
1 small onion, chopped
Salt and pepper to taste

This recipe is perfect for Sunday brunch at home or for taking for a Georgia football tailgate breakfast in a reheatable foil pan.

Combine everything in a large bowl and place in a greased baking dish. Bake at 350° for about 45 minutes.

Good Morning Breakfast Casserole

1 pound ground sausage
½ cup chopped onion
2 cups seasoned croutons
1 cup shredded Cheddar cheese
1 (4-ounce) can mushroom pieces, drained
6 eggs, beaten
2½ cups milk, divided
Salt, pepper and dry mustard
1 (10¾-ounce) can cream of mushroom soup

Easy to mix it up the night before then bake the next morning.

Brown sausage with onions; drain and set aside. Place croutons in a 9x13-inch dish sprayed with nonstick vegetable spray. Top with cheese, mushrooms and reserved sausage. Combine eggs with 2 cups milk; add salt, pepper and dry mustard to taste. Pour over sausage. Cover and refrigerate overnight. Combine soup with remaining ½ cup milk; spread over top. Bake 1 hour (or until set) at 325°. Serves 6 to 8.

Country Ham & Grits Quiche

1 cup cooked grits
2 tablespoons butter
12 ounces country ham, cooked and cut into bite-size pieces
1 (9-inch) frozen deep-dish pie crust
5 eggs, beaten
2 tablespoons whipping cream
¼ teaspoon black pepper
1 cup shredded Cheddar cheese

Preheat oven to 375°. Combine grits and butter, stir until butter is melted and grits are smooth and creamy. Add country ham and mix well. Pour mixture into pie shell, set aside. In medium bowl, beat together eggs, whipping cream, pepper and cheese. Pour over grits mixture. Bake about 30 to 40 minutes or until knife inserted near center comes out clean. Let stand 5 minutes before serving.

Jewell Hutto, Executive Director, Georgia Egg Commission

Hot and Cheesy Baked Grits

1½ cups quick grits (not instant),
    plus ingredients to cook per directions
1 stick (½ cup) margarine
1 pound processed cheese, cubed
1 can Ro-Tel tomatoes (tomatoes with chilies), drained
3 eggs, beaten

Cook grits per directions on package until thick. Add margarine and cheese; stir until melted. Add drained tomatoes and eggs; mix well. Pour into a 9x13-inch glass baking dish treated with nonstick spray. Bake 90 minutes at 275°.

Grits 'n Sausage Breakfast Bake

1 cup uncooked grits
1 stick (½ cup) butter
1 pound ground sausage
⅔ cup diced onion
1 can green chilies
3 eggs, beaten
2 cups shredded Cheddar cheese
1 teaspoon paprika

Some people say grits were invented in Georgia. Others say, they may not have been invented here, but folks in Georgia surely perfected them.

Cook grits as directed on package; stir in butter to melt. Brown sausage; drain. Combine all ingredients in a greased baking dish and bake at 325° about 45 minutes. Top with additional cheese if desired. Serve hot.

Confetti-Style Scrambled Tortillas

6 large eggs
¼ cup milk
½ teaspoon salt
⅛ teaspoon pepper
2 tablespoons butter, melted
Shredded cheese
Tortilla shells
½ cup salsa

Beat eggs, milk, salt and pepper with a whisk until mixed well. Melt butter in a skillet over medium heat; cook eggs (scrambled). Top with cheese to taste. Serve wrapped in tortilla shells with salsa on the side for dipping.

Peachy French Toast

1 cup packed brown sugar
1 stick (½ cup) butter or margarine
2 tablespoons water
1 (29-ounce) can sliced peaches, drained
12 to 14 (1-inch-thick) slices French bread
5 large eggs, beaten
1½ cups milk
3 teaspoons vanilla extract

Mix the night before for a quick breakfast the next morning.

Melt brown sugar and butter in a small saucepan over medium-low heat until melted. Add water and cook over medium heat until thick (about 5 minutes). Pour into a 9x13-inch glass baking dish; cool 10 minutes (no more). Place peaches over sauce; cover with bread. Whisk eggs, milk and vanilla; pour over bread. Cover and refrigerate overnight. Preheat oven to 350°. Bake, uncovered, 40 minutes or until set and top is golden. (If top browns before the dish is set, cover with foil for remaining cook time.) Serves 6 to 8.

Quick Pecan Honey Sticky Buns

⅓ cup firmly packed brown sugar
⅔ stick butter, melted
1 tablespoon honey
½ cup chopped pecans
1 can large refrigerated biscuits

Sometimes you just need a good batch of sticky buns. Here is an easy recipe that only takes a few minutes from start to finish.

In a saucepan, combine brown sugar, butter and honey. Cook on medium heat until well blended. Pour into a nonstick 9-inch round baking pan and sprinkle with pecans. Arrange biscuits, with sides touching, in single layer over pecans. Bake at 350° about 15 minutes, or until biscuits are golden brown. Remove from oven and carefully place a clean plate over top of pan. Turn over and allow biscuits to drop upside down onto plate with pecans and sauce mix now on top. Serve warm.

Georgia Honey-Pecan French Toast

Toast

4 eggs, beaten
1 cup milk
2 tablespoons vanilla extract
1 tablespoon dark brown sugar
8 to 10 slices Texas-style toast

Topping

1 stick (½ cup) butter, melted
½ cup dark brown sugar
½ cup chopped pecans
⅓ cup Georgia honey

Combine eggs, milk, vanilla and brown sugar in a large bowl; dip each piece toast in mixture. Cook on a hot griddle until golden brown. Mix topping ingredients in a bowl and heat in microwave. Drizzle over cooked French toast.

Cloudland Canyon State Park
Rising Fawn

Kent Whitaker

Easy-Baked Honey Bran Muffins

4 cups whole-bran cereal
2 cups pineapple juice
2 cups golden raisins
1 cup packed brown sugar
½ cup vegetable oil
½ cup honey
5 eggs, beaten
2 cups all-purpose flour
2 teaspoons baking soda
1 teaspoon salt

Combine all ingredients in a large bowl. Cover and chill for an hour or so. Batter will thicken as cereal absorbs some of the moisture. Fill greased muffin cups about ¾ full and bake at 375° for about 25 minutes. Cool slightly before serving.

Hahira Honeybee Festival

Hahira • First week of October

Each year Hahira and the Honey Bee Committee's "Busy Bees" prepare for the Honey Bee Festival held the first week of October. The week long extravaganza, begun by Mamie Sorrell and Adeline Landrum in 1981, includes arts, crafts, a beauty pageant and parade. For the past 25 years, the festival has been one of the best in the southeast with more than 20,000 visitors.

229.794.3097 • www.hahira.ga.us

Peach Muffins

⅓ cup butter, softened
½ cup sugar
1 egg, beaten
1½ cups self-rising flour
¼ teaspoon ground nutmeg (optional)
½ cup milk
½ cup chopped Georgia peaches

Topping

½ cup sugar
1 teaspoon ground cinnamon
½ cup butter, melted

Preheat oven to 350°. Cream butter and ½ cup sugar; mix in egg. Combine flour and nutmeg. Stir flour mixture into butter mixture alternately with milk. Stir in peaches. Fill greased muffin cups ⅔ full. Bake 20 to 25 minutes. Combine ½ cup sugar with cinnamon. When muffins are cooked, immediately dip tops into melted butter then into cinnamon-sugar mixture. YUM!

Tasty Georgia Blueberry Muffins

2½ cups all-purpose flour
½ cup sugar
2½ teaspoons baking powder
¼ teaspoon salt
1 teaspoon cinnamon
1 cup milk
2 eggs, beaten
½ cup butter, melted
1½ cups frozen blueberries, thawed and drained
Butter for topping
Powdered sugar for topping

Combine dry ingredients; stir in milk, eggs and melted butter. Spoon into prepared muffin tins or paper muffin cups filling about ⅔ full. Bake at 400° for 20 to 25 minutes. Remove from oven and spread a small amount of butter over each muffin. Allow to cool slightly then sprinkle with powdered sugar before serving.

Sweet Buttered Cornbread Muffins

1 cup unbleached all-purpose flour
1 cup cornmeal
5 tablespoons sugar
2 teaspoons baking powder
½ teaspoon salt
1 cup milk
⅓ cup oil
1 large egg, beaten
4 tablespoons (½ stick) butter, melted
1 tablespoon honey

They say there are two kids of people in Georgia, those who like their cornbread sweet and those who don't. These delicious muffins are sure to please at least half the people.

Combine all ingredients except butter and honey in a large bowl and mix well. Batter should be slightly clumpy. Pour into muffin tin and bake at 400° until golden brown. Combine melted butter and honey in a small bowl and spoon a small amount over each muffin just before removing from oven.

Sweet Cornbread Hoe Cakes

1½ cups yellow cornmeal
1 cup flour
¼ cup sugar
1 tablespoon brown sugar
½ teaspoon salt
2 teaspoons baking powder
½ teaspoon baking soda
¼ cup shortening
1 egg, beaten
1 cup buttermilk

Combine dry ingredients in a large bowl; stir in shortening. Add egg and buttermilk; mix well. Bake as 1 large hoe cake in the oven at 400° for 15 to 20 minutes, or for small, pan-fried hoe cakes add additional milk for a thinner batter and cook like you would a pancake.

Iron Skillet Cracklin' Cornbread

Vegetable shortening
1¼ cups cornmeal
½ teaspoon salt
⅔ cup all-purpose flour
1 egg, beaten
2 tablespoons sugar

1 cup milk
1 tablespoon baking powder
¼ cup salad oil
3 tablespoons mayonnaise
½ cup chopped onion
½ cup real bacon bits

Preheat oven to 425°. Spoon a dollop of vegetable shortening in a cast iron skillet, and place in oven during preheating time. Combine all ingredients in a large bowl and pour batter into skillet. Bake 20 to 25 minutes or until golden brown. Slice and serve hot.

Sour Cream Cornbread

4 eggs
1 pint sour cream
1 cup vegetable oil
2 cups self-rising cornmeal mix
1 small can cream-style corn
½ teaspoon salt

Preheat oven to 400°. Beat eggs; add sour cream and mix well. Add oil and mix well. Stir in cornmeal, corn and salt until blended well. Pour into a greased 9x13-inch glass baking dish. Bake 30 to 35 minutes. Serves 12.

Fresh Baked Bread

2½ cups flour
¾ cup rolled oats
1 teaspoon salt
1 package dry yeast
1 cup water
⅓ cup honey
¼ cup butter
1 egg, beaten

Nothing smells better than homemade bread baking. Try this easy yeast-bread recipe for a no-fuss, Southern-style fresh-baked loaf of bread.

In a large bowl, combine flour, oats, salt and yeast; mix well. In a small saucepan, heat water, honey and butter until butter is melted. Add to dry ingredients along with egg; fold with heavy spoon. Cover and allow to rise 25 minutes. Stir mix down again, cover and let rise an additional 20 minutes. Pour into a prepared loaf pan and bake at 375° for 35 minutes. Cool on wire rack.

Vidalia Onion Beer Bread

3 cups self-rising flour
¼ cup brown sugar
1 teaspoon baking powder
½ teaspoon salt
½ teaspoon onion powder
¾ teaspoon Italian seasoning
1 small Vidalia onion, diced
1 can beer
¼ cup melted butter

Mix dry ingredients, seasonings and onion in a bowl. Pour beer in slowly. Pour batter into a prepared baking pan. Top with the melted butter. Bake at 350° for 35 to 45 minutes. Allow to cool before slicing.

Kevin Lecroy, West Georgia University

Buttermilk Pinch Rolls

1 cup thick buttermilk
1 teaspoon sugar
¼ teaspoon baking soda
3 tablespoons shortening
1 package active dry yeast
3 cups sifted all-purpose flour
1 teaspoon baking powder
1 teaspoon salt

Heat buttermilk over low heat until luke warm. In a large bowl, combine buttermilk, sugar, baking soda and shortening until mixed well. Add yeast and stir to dissolve. Add flour, baking powder and salt; mix gently. Cover and allow dough to rise about 15 minutes. Knead dough 5 to 8 minutes until smooth and pliable. Roll dough into a long tube shape and pinch into 1- to 1½-inch rolls. Place in greased baking pan or on greased baking sheet; cover with a dampened cloth and let rise until double in size. Bake at 400° for 15 to 20 minutes.

Butter-Dipped Breadsticks

2 cans refrigerated dinner rolls or biscuits
1 stick (½ cup) melted butter
Cinnamon and sugar (or garlic powder and Italian seasoning)

Open cans and roll bread into sticks. Dip in butter and roll in a mixture of cinnamon and sugar if serving for breakfast or a mixture of garlic powder and Italian seasoning if serving for dinner. Bake at 325° until golden brown.

Fry Bread

4 cups all-purpose flour
1 teaspoon salt
2 teaspoons baking powder
2 cups water
Vegetable oil for frying

Mix flour, salt and baking powder in a large bowl. Gradually stir in water until dough is soft and no longer sticking to bowl. Knead dough on lightly floured flat surface at least 5 minutes. Return dough to bowl and cover with a clean towel; let sit 30 minutes. Shape dough into egg-size balls; roll each on lightly floured surface to a thickness of ½ inch. Slap each from hand to hand as you would pizza dough until it is 8 to 12 inches in diameter. Heat about 1½ inches oil in a large frying pan over medium heat. Cook pieces, turning once until bread is golden brown. Drain on paper towels; serve immediately. Fry Bread is excellent with butter and honey, fruit toppings, and/or smothered with all of your favorite taco garnishes which makes for the famous "Indian Taco."

Note: If making lots of Fry Bread in deep fryer, it is important to change oil when it starts to get dark or burned. Working the dough at least 5 minutes and clean oil is what makes for good Fry Bread.

Chipa Wolf
Annual Etowah Valley Indian Festival

Etowah Valley Indian Festival
Sam Smith Park at Milam Farm
Cartersville • October

Enjoy this great festival at Milam Farm Park, near the native lands of the Etowah Indian Mounds State Historic Site. Celebrate Cartersville's rich Native American heritage with traditional dance, music, native foods, storytelling and educators of traditional crafts and skills. Shop for authentic crafts: cornshuck dolls, gourd carvings, native beads, jewelry, baskets and more. Enjoy an evening concert, Warriors on Horseback, native dancers, primitive cooking demonstrations and much more.

770.735.6275 • www.rthunder.com

Fall Phyllos

1 (16-ounce) box phyllo dough sheets
1 cup margarine, melted
1 (4.6-ounce) box broccoli & cheese rice mix, prepared
4 ounces smoked ham, finely chopped
5 tablespoons garden vegetable-flavored cream cheese
2 eggs, beaten
½ teaspoon black pepper
1 (0.9-ounce) package hollandaise sauce, plus ingredients
   to prepare according to directions on package

Preheat oven to 350°. Place 2 sheets phyllo dough onto wax paper or cutting board. Using a basting brush, lightly brush margarine on top. Starting from the end, fold to the center and brush with margarine. Fold again and brush with margarine. Gently place dough into an ungreased fluted muffin pan, with margarine side up. Gently press dough into pan to fit mold with corners placed outside top of mold. Repeat until muffin pan is full. Combine broccoli and cheese rice, ham, cream cheese, eggs and pepper. Spoon into phyllo dough cups filling each to the top. Bake 20 minutes or until mixture is set. While Fall Phyllos are baking, prepare hollandaise sauce. Keep warm until ready to use. When done, remove muffins from oven. Plate each muffin and serve with a teaspoon of hollandaise on top.

Jewell Hutto, Executive Director
Georgia Egg Commission

Etowah Indian Mounds Historic Site
Cartersville, Georgia

Peach Bread

½ cup butter or margarine, softened
1 cup sugar
3 eggs
2¾ cups all-purpose flour
1½ teaspoons baking powder
½ teaspoon baking soda
1 teaspoon salt
1½ teaspoons ground cinnamon
2 cups sliced fresh peaches
3 tablespoons frozen orange juice
    concentrate, thawed
1 teaspoon vanilla extract

Cream butter and sugar. Add eggs, 1 at a time, beating well after each addition. In a separate bowl, combine flour, baking powder, baking soda, salt and cinnamon. Add combined dry ingredients to creamed mixture alternately with peaches, beginning and ending with flour mixture. Stir in orange juice concentrate and vanilla. Pour batter into a greased and floured 9x5-inch loaf pan. Bake at 350° for 1 hour or until wooden pick inserted in center comes out clean. Cool in pan 10 minutes. Remove from loaf pan and cool completely before serving.

Easy-Baked Pecan Monkey Bread

3 to 4 cans small refrigerated biscuits
1 stick (½ cup) butter, melted
½ cup sugar
½ cup brown sugar
1½ tablespoons cinnamon
½ cup chopped Georgia pecans

Cut each biscuit in half. Melt butter in microwave. In a large zip-close bag, combine white sugar, brown sugar, cinnamon and pecans. Dip biscuit pieces in butter. Put biscuits, a few at a time, into bag and gently shake to coat. Stack pieces in a prepared bundt pan or loaf pan. Pour any left-over butter and sugar mix over bread. Bake at 350° until biscuit pieces are fully cooked and top is golden brown.

Quick Mix Banana Nut Bread

2 ripe bananas, mashed
⅔ cup sugar
2⅔ cups biscuit mix
½ teaspoon brown sugar
¼ cup milk
3 tablespoons vegetable oil
½ teaspoon vanilla extract
3 eggs, beaten
½ cup chopped nuts

Combine all ingredients in a large bowl. Pour into a greased loaf pan. Bake at 350° 45 to 50 minutes. Cool 10 minutes then remove from pan and allow to cool on a wire rack.

Pumpkin Nut Bread

2 cups sifted all-purpose flour
2 teaspoons baking powder
½ teaspoon baking soda
1 teaspoon cinnamon
½ teaspoon nutmeg
1 teaspoon salt
1 can pumpkin meat
1 cup sugar
¼ cup brown sugar
2 eggs, beaten
½ cup milk
¼ cup butter, softened
½ cup chopped walnuts
½ cup chopped pecans

Canned pumpkin never tasted so good!

In a large bowl, combine all ingredients. Pour batter into a greased loaf pan (or 2 small loaf pans). Bake in 350° oven 45 to 55 minutes.

Georgia

Salads

Mixed Caesar Salad

Salad

1 bag mixed lettuce greens
1 cup croutons
Parmesan cheese to taste
¼ cup sunflower seeds

Dressing

½ cup olive oil
½ tablespoon minced garlic
1 teaspoon Worcestershire sauce
1 teaspoon lemon juice
1 teaspoon vinegar

Combine salad ingredients in serving bowl. Combine dressing ingredients in a bowl and blend. Spoon over salad and serve chilled.

Simple Spinach Salad

Salad

8 cups baby spinach leaves
½ cup chopped celery
2 Granny Smith apples, chopped

Dressing

½ cup vanilla yogurt
1 teaspoon sugar
¼ cup orange juice
⅛ teaspoon salt

Combine spinach, celery and apples in large bowl; toss gently. In separate bowl, combine dressing ingredients; mix well. Drizzle over salad and toss to coat. Makes 4 servings.

Georgia

Peach Apricot Green Salad

1 large ripe peach, thinly sliced
1 fresh apricot, thinly sliced (or canned slices)
2 tablespoons fresh lemon juice
2 tablespoons orange juice
6 tablespoons olive oil
3 tablespoons Caesar dressing
1 bag mixed greens
Salt and pepper
5 tablespoons feta cheese
Garlic-flavored croutons (optional)

Lightly toss peaches and apricots with lemon and orange juice. Stir in olive oil and dressing. Mix in greens; salt and pepper to taste. Top with Feta cheese and croutons to taste.

Asparagus Salad with Dijon Dressing

¼ cup mayonnaise
1 tablespoon Dijon mustard
1 teaspoon apple cider vinegar
Dash Tabasco
1 head green leafy lettuce, rinsed and chopped
1 (15-ounce) can asparagus spears, drained
2 eggs, hard-boiled and chopped
2 tomatoes, peeled and chopped

Combine mayonnaise, mustard, vinegar and Tabasco to make Dijon dressing. Chill at least 1 hour and up to 24 hours. Place lettuce in 4 serving bowls or plates. Top with equal amounts asparagus, eggs and tomatoes. Serve with Dijon Dressing on the side. Serves 4.

Orange Marinated Chopped Chicken Salad

8 chicken tenders
1 cup plus 3 tablespoons orange juice, divided
1 small Vidalia onion, chopped
2 teaspoons ground ginger
Oil
1 bag mixed salad greens
1 cup crumpled cheese
½ cup dried cranberries
Vinaigrette dressing
Crushed black pepper

Marinate chicken in orange juice, onions and ginger overnight or as long as possible. In a skillet, using a small amount of oil, cook chicken and onions. When chicken is almost done, add 3 tablespoons orange juice; continue to cook until juice cooks dry and chicken browns. In a bowl, combine salad greens, cheese and cranberries. Serve topped with hot chicken, dressing and crushed black pepper.

Taste of Alpharetta
Alpharetta • May

The largest "Taste of" festival in the South! Dine at over 70 restaurants in one unforgettable night that's become an annual tradition for 70,000 families, foodies and festival-goers. Sample delicious appetizers, entrees and desserts, experience the new Culinary Arts area featuring chef's competition, cooking demonstrations and exhibits. Bring a blanket to the new concert lawn for live jazz, rock and contemporary music. Play at the Kids Zone or Fun Zone for older kids. Party with 12 metro radio stations. Visit the new Community Corner.

678.297.6000 • www.alpharetta.ga.us

Grilled Chicken & Georgia Apple Salad

3 cups diced North Georgia apples
3 cups diced grilled chicken, cooled
1 cup chopped Vidalia onion
1 cup chopped celery
¼ cup dark raisins
¼ cup chopped pecans
3 tablespoons mayonnaise

Combine all ingredients. Add additional mayonnaise if needed for your taste. Mix well and chill. Serve cold.

Chunky Almond Chicken Salad

3 cups cooked chunked chicken
2 to 3 stalks celery, chopped
2 carrots, chopped
⅓ cup chopped Vidalia onion
⅓ cup chopped almonds
½ tablespoon minced garlic
1 teaspoon salt
1 teaspoon black pepper
Mayonnaise
Yellow mustard (optional)

This is one of my favorite chicken salad recipes. I like to chop the ingredients in larger pieces for a chunky and crunchy chicken salad.

Place everything except mayonnaise and mustard in a large bowl. Stir in 3 tablespoons mayonnaise and, if desired, ½ tablespoon mustard. Add additional mayo and/or mustard to taste. Mix well and chill before serving.

Country Carrot Salad

6 to 8 peeled carrots, finely chopped
1 cup broken broccoli
½ cup raisins
½ cup chopped pecans
Mayonnaise to taste

In a large bowl, combine carrots, broccoli, raisins and chopped pecans. Add a spoonful of mayo; stir. Continue to add mayo until you get the mixture you desire. Chill and serve.

Southern-Style Sweet Pea Salad

1 can sweet peas
¼ cup thinly sliced and diced cucumber
¼ cup thinly sliced and diced onion
2 to 3 sweet pickles, chopped
1 teaspoon dill weed
2 tablespoons mayonnaise

Blend all vegetables together gently to avoid crushing the canned peas. Sprinkle dill weed over salad and stir in mayonnaise. Refrigerate at least 1 hour before serving.

Georgia

Low Fat Broccoli Salad

3 cups broken broccoli
2 cups shredded raw cabbage
⅓ cup fat-free mayonnaise
¼ cup cider vinegar

Dash artificial sweetener
2 teaspoons celery seeds
1 can chopped water chestnuts, drained
3 tablespoons sunflower seeds

Combine all ingredients in a large bowl; mix well. Chill and serve.

Note: Increase broccoli and leave out cabbage, if desired.

Broccoli and Cauliflower Crunchy Salad

Salad
4 cups small broccoli pieces
2 cups small-chopped cauliflower tops
½ cup Vidalia onion, chopped
2 stalks celery, chopped
½ cup raisins
1 cup chopped walnuts or Georgia pecans

Dressing
1 cup mayonnaise
¼ cup vinegar
¼ cup sugar

Topping
1 cup Asian noodles
⅔ cup real bacon bits

Combine salad ingredients in a bowl; toss well. Add in dressing ingredients; mix well. Chill about 30 minutes. Serve topped with Asian noodles and bacon bits.

Wild Georgia Shrimp Salad

Green Mayonnaise

½ cup mayonnaise
¼ cup minced onion
½ cup minced parsley
¼ cup minced cilantro

Shrimp

1 pound boiled Wild Georgia Shrimp, peeled, deveined and coarsely chopped
Salt and pepper to taste
1 celery stalk, minced
1 medium red bell pepper, minced
1 small onion, minced
1 boiled egg, diced
½ teaspoon paprika

Combine all Green Mayonnaise ingredients in a large bowl; mix well. Add remaining ingredients, except paprika; mix well. Top with a sprinkle of paprika. Chill before serving.

Courtesy of Catherine Wallace
Submitted by Wild Georgia Shrimp

Georgia shrimper Catherine Wallace makes this delicious cold salad with plain mayonnaise, but this recipe gives an extra kick with "green mayonnaise," spiked with onion, parsley and cilantro.

National Grits Festival

Warwick • April

The annual National Grits Festival is more than 10 years old and attracts thousands of attendees each year. Featuring the famous Quaker® Grits Breakfast, art show, live entertainment, food vendors, craft dealers, pony ride and much more, the festival is guaranteed fun for people of all ages. Events unique to the festival include the corn-shelling event, Quaker® Grits eating competition, and the famous "Roll in the Quaker® Instant Grits" event where participants roll around in a cattle trough full of cooked Quaker® Instant Grits. The festival is family-oriented, free event. Everyone is invited for a day of southern food, fun and entertainment.

229.395.4737 • www.gritsfest.com

Roasted Pecan-Topped Vegetable Salad

2 medium zucchini, chopped
2 medium summer squash, chopped
1 red onion, diced
4 medium tomatoes, diced
¾ cup chopped pecans

2 to 3 tablespoons olive oil
½ teaspoon salt
2 teaspoons Balsamic vinegar
4 cups bagged salad greens, rinsed
Parmesan cheese

In medium bowl, toss zucchini, squash, onion and tomatoes with chopped pecans, olive oil and salt. Spread mixture in a single layer on a large cookie sheet coated with nonstick spray. Roast veggies in a 375° oven about 10 minutes. Turn once and cook a few minutes more. To serve, mix salad greens and vinegar; divide among plates, spoon equal amounts roasted veggies over greens and top with a dash of Parmesan cheese.

Zesty Vidalia Onion and Cucumber Salad

3 cups peeled, seeded and sliced cucumbers
1½ cups sliced Vidalia onions
½ cup grated carrots
½ cup white vinegar
¼ cup sugar
2 tablespoons water
2 tablespoons chopped fresh dill or 1 tablespoon dried dill weed
½ teaspoon salt
¼ teaspoon ground black pepper
½ cup chopped Georgia pecans

In a medium bowl, toss together cucumbers, onions and carrot; set aside. In a liquid measuring cup, combine vinegar, sugar, water, dill, salt and pepper. Pour over cucumber mixture; toss to coat. Top with pecans and serve.

Hot German Potato Salad

4 pounds potatoes
4 slices bacon, cooked (with drippings)
1 medium onion, diced
2 whole dilled pickles, diced
1 teaspoon pickle juice
1 teaspoon vegetable oil
1 teaspoon cider vinegar (more or less to taste; this adds the tangy taste)
1 teaspoon hot water
5 eggs, boiled and sliced
Salt and pepper to taste

Boil potatoes, in skins, until done. Peel and slice while still hot (do not allow them to cool). Combine with remaining ingredients. Set aside at room temperature 1 hour before serving.

Recipe from Elka Snyder
Courtesy of Oktoberfest • Helen, Georgia

Oktoberfest
Helen • October

Helen's Oktoberfest festival begins Friday evening with great gospel entertainment and a leisurely dinner in the shady city park On Saturday, there are lots of things to do and see for the whole family. The parade steps out at 10 am, led by the Teddy Bear Parade. The festival mascot, Reynolds S. Berry leads the little ones and their teddy bears along the short route on foot or decorated tricycles, wagons or other conveyances. The Grand Parade follows and should be a real crowd pleaser. After the parade passes by, the kids go to the bandstand for the Teddy Bear Picnic.

1.800.858.8027 • www.helenchamber.com

Tater & Vidalia Salad

4 to 5 pounds potatoes
1 medium Vidalia onion
6 eggs, boiled peeled and chopped
⅔ cup mayonnaise
½ cup mustard
⅓ cup sweet relish
Salt and pepper to taste
½ cup real bacon bits

Any decent cook-out in the Peach State includes a great tater salad. This recipe is outstanding with Vidalia onions and bacon bits.

Clean potatoes and peel, if desired. Cook potatoes whole until tender; cut into bite-size pieces. Combine all ingredients in a large bowl, cover and chill before serving.

Octoberfest Mural
Helen, Georgia

Kent Whitaker

Seven Layer Slaw

2 cups prepared coleslaw mix, divided
2 cups shredded carrots, divided
2 cups prepared broccoli slaw mix, divided
1 yellow bell pepper, chopped
1 cup mayonnaise
¼ cup sugar
¼ cup water
2 tablespoons pepper

Spread ½ coleslaw mix into bottom of large clear glass bowl. Layer on ½ carrots, ½ broccoli slaw, then ½ bell pepper. Whisk together mayonnaise, sugar, water and pepper; pour ½ over slaw. Repeat vegetable layers; pour remaining dressing over top. Cover and refrigerate at least 3 hours or overnight. Toss before serving. Makes 6 servings.

Shredded Coleslaw

3 to 4 cups shredded cabbage
1 cup shredded red cabbage
½ green bell pepper, thinly sliced (optional)
⅔ cup red wine vinegar
¼ cup olive oil
2 tablespoons sugar
2 teaspoons salt
½ teaspoon celery seeds
¼ teaspoon ground black pepper

Combine everything in a bowl and mix well. Cover and chill before serving.

Creamy Sweet Slaw

½ head cabbage, finely diced
1 small carrot, minced
3 to 4 tablespoons mayo
1 teaspoon sugar
½ teaspoon apple cider vinegar, if desired
Dash black pepper

Combine all in a large bowl, cover and chill before serving.

Georgia Peach Slaw

2 pounds ripe peaches, pitted and chopped
1 small head cabbage, shredded
1 teaspoon salt
½ cup mayonnaise
3 tablespoons apple cider vinegar
2 tablespoons honey
1 teaspoon Dijon mustard
½ teaspoon freshly ground pepper
4 scallions, chopped
1 cup toasted pecans, coarsely chopped

Coat peaches with cooking spray and bake about 5 minutes in a hot oven on broil. Cook just enough to barely brown edges. Remove from oven and combine with remaining ingredients. Toss to coat evenly and serve.

Orzo Black Bean Salad

8 ounces orzo pasta
1 can black beans, rinsed and drained
1 can whole-kernel corn, rinsed and drained
1 small red bell, chopped
1 small Vidalia onion, chopped
¼ teaspoon salt
1 teaspoon olive oil
2 tablespoons lemon juice
2½ tablespoons olive oil
½ teaspoon ground cumin
½ teaspoon black pepper
1 cup prepared salsa
2 tablespoons cilantro
2 tablespoons parsley
⅓ cup chopped Georgia pecans
Salad greens

Cook orzo per directions on box. Before draining add in black beans, corn, bell pepper, and onion. Cook about 5 minutes more; drain. In a large bowl, combine orzo mixture with remaining ingredients. Serve warm or chilled over a small amount of mixed salad greens.

Chopped Tomato Pasta Salad

1 package angel hair pasta
½ cup zesty Italian dressing
2 tomatoes, chopped
¼ cup grated Parmesan cheese

Bring a large pot of lightly salted water to a boil. Add pasta and cook 8 to 10 minutes or until al dente; drain and place into a large serving bowl. Toss with dressing and tomatoes. Top with Parmesan and serve.

Frosted Grape Salad

2 pounds seedless green grapes
2 pounds seedless purple or red grapes
1 (8-ounce) carton sour cream
1 (8-ounce) package cream cheese, softened
½ cup sugar
1 cup chopped almonds
¾ cup packed brown sugar

Wash grapes, remove from stems, and allow to dry completely. Mix sour cream, cream cheese and sugar. Carefully mix in grapes by hand. Refrigerate until ready to serve. Just before serving, combine almonds and brown sugar; sprinkle over Frosted Grape Salad.

Peachy Fruit Salad

1 (20-ounce) can peach pie filling
2 bananas, sliced
2 cups green grapes
1 (11-ounce) can mandarin oranges, drained
1 (20-ounce) can pineapple chunks, drained
2 cups miniature marshmallows
1 cup chopped pecans

Combine all ingredients and toss gently. Refrigerate until ready to serve.

Millionaire Peach Salad

1 (8-ounce) package cream cheese, softened
1 cup powdered sugar
1 (12-ounce) carton Cool Whip
1 small box peach jello
 2 cans peaches, drain and reserve juice
2 cups miniature marshmallows
1 cup chopped pecans

Combine cream cheese and powdered sugar with mixer until smooth. Stir in Cool Whip then dry jello. Stir in peaches and ⅛ cup reserved juice (any remaining juice may be discarded). Add marshmallows and pecans; stir. Chill several hours or overnight. Delicious as a side dish, but rich enough for dessert.

Soups, Stews, Chilis & Chowders

Potato Cheese Soup

3 chicken bullion cubes
5 cups water
2 carrots, finely chopped
3 cups red potatoes, cubed
1 can cream of chicken soup
½ pound Velveeta, cubed

Dissolve bullion cubes in water and bring to a boil. Add carrots and cook 20 minutes. Add potatoes; cook an additional 20 minutes. Add cream of chicken soup and Velveeta. Heat until cheese is melted. Serve with cornbread.

Scott Herpst
Walker County Messenger

Cheddar Cheese Soup

1 small onion, minced
4 tablespoons butter
¼ cup flour
2 cans chicken broth
1 can Cheddar cheese soup
2 cups milk

1 cup sour cream
1 cup shredded Cheddar cheese
Salt and pepper to taste
2 cups evaporated milk
1 stalk celery, finely chopped

Brown onions in butter. Combine all ingredients in a large nonstick pot; cook over low heat, stirring frequently, until cheese is melted and soup begins to bubble. Thin with additional milk or water when necessary. Serve hot with a garnish of paprika and parsley and crackers on the side.

Country Hot Sausage & Tater Soup

1 pound hot ground sausage
1 Vidalia onion, chopped
2 stalks celery, chopped
3 tablespoons butter
¼ cup flour
½ cup chopped green onions
1 tablespoon parsley
1 teaspoon basil
½ teaspoon garlic power
½ teaspoon chili powder
1 teaspoon salt
½ tablespoon black pepper
3 cans chicken broth
2 cups water
5 potatoes, peeled and diced
1½ cups heavy cream

In a large skillet, brown sausage with onion, celery and butter; drain excess fat. In a large pot, combine sausage with remaining ingredients and cover. Cook over medium-low heat until potatoes are cooked. Stir often to break potatoes up into smaller pieces. (Some prefer the potatoes almost mashed.) The soup should thicken as it cooks. Use milk to thin or flour to thicken as desired. Serve hot.

Ham & Shrimp Jambalaya Soup

½ pound salad shrimp
½ pound ham, finely diced
1 cup chopped onion
1 red bell pepper, finely diced
½ tablespoon minced garlic
1 tablespoon olive oil

1 can stewed tomatoes
1 can chicken broth
3½ cups water
1 tablespoon Cajun seasoning
1 tablespoon butter
1½ cups instant rice

In a nonstick skillet, brown shrimp, ham, onion, bell pepper and garlic in olive oil about 5 minutes or until tender. Don't overcook; you just want to give everything a quick golden edge. Combine all ingredients in a large pot and simmer over medium heat for 30 minutes. Depending on how thick you want your soup, you can add a bit of milk or water. Serve hot in bowls. For a garnish, gently place a single cracker on the surface of the soup and drizzle a small amount of hot sauce on the cracker.

Rock Shrimp Festival
St. Marys • October

Historic downtown St. Marys is home to the annual Rock Shrimp Festival with lots of fun for the whole family. Sponsored by the Kiwanis Club, the festival includes 5k/10k races, parade, entertainment, street dance, food concessions, arts and crafts booths and of course delicious rock shrimp dinners.

800.868.8687 • www.stmaryswelcome.com

Shrimp Creole

2 strips smoked bacon, cut to ½-inch pieces
1 pound andouille or smoked sausage, thinly sliced
1 pound Wild Georgia Shrimp, peeled and deveined
1 cup chopped onion
½ cup chopped green bell pepper
¼ cup flour
3 garlic cloves, minced
1 (15-ounce) can chopped tomatoes
½ cup tomato sauce
½ cup white wine
½ teaspoon Creole seasoning
1 teaspoon Worcestershire sauce
Salt, pepper and Tabasco® to taste

My friend John Wallace at Wild Georgia Shrimp gave me this recipe which came from shrimper Billy Nelson. Billy has been fishing for 33 years in the Atlantic and the Gulf of Mexico and is a lifelong resident of McIntosh County, Georgia.

In a large, heavy pot, sauté bacon and sausage over medium heat until they begin to color. Remove and reserve. In the same fat, quickly sauté shrimp just until they turn opaque; salt and pepper to taste. Remove and reserve. Add onion and bell pepper to the pot. Cook vegetables until soft and they begin to brown. Gradually add flour while stirring. Cook over low heat, stirring constantly, until a medium brown roux (the color of peanut butter) is formed. Add garlic; stir to mix. Add tomatoes, tomato sauce, wine, Creole seasoning, Worcestershire and salt, pepper and Tabasco to taste; break tomatoes with the back of a spoon. Bring to a boil, turn heat down and simmer 20 minutes. Add a little chicken broth or hot water if too thick. Add reserved bacon, sausage and shrimp, and simmer just long enough to heat through. Serve over rice.

Courtesy of Billy Nelson
Submitted by Wild Georgia Shrimp

Cream of Mushroom Bacon Soup

⅓ cup butter
½ pound mushrooms, finely chopped
¾ cup flour
1 can beef or chicken stock
½ cup water
½ cup milk
½ cup sour cream
1 tablespoon salt
1 tablespoon Worcestershire sauce
1 teaspoon lemon juice
½ cup real bacon bits
Parsley

A standard soup made easy... and creamy... and topped with bacon!

Melt butter in a skillet; add mushrooms. Cook until brown. In a large pot, combine mushrooms, flour, meat stock and water. Stir over medium heat until flour is dissolved. Add milk, sour cream, salt, Worcestershire and lemon juice; stir to mix well. Cook over medium-low about 30 minutes. Serve hot topped with bacon bits and parsley.

Easy Can a Can Veggie Beef Soup

1 to 2 cups water
½ teaspoon salt
1 can store-bought Brunswick or beef stew
2 cans mixed vegetables
1 can tomato sauce
½ cup milk

In a large pot, combine 1 cup water with remaining ingredients; simmer 20 minutes over medium heat adding more water if needed. Serve hot with crackers.

Country Hopping John and Greens Soup

1 ham bone or fat back
4 tablespoons hot sauce
2 medium Vidalia onions, diced
1 can black-eyed peas
1 can store-bought chili with beans
6 cups water
½ cup uncooked brown rice
1 red bell pepper, chopped
1 green bell pepper, chopped
Salt and pepper to taste
4 cups cleaned and finely chopped mustard greens

In a stockpot, combine ham, hot sauce, onions, black-eyed peas, chili and water; cook over medium heat for 30 minutes. Stir in rice and peppers; season to taste with salt and pepper. Add more water if needed. When rice is done stir in greens and cook about 10 minutes to warm greens. Serve hot. You can substitute spinach, if desired, for the mustard greens.

Sweet Onion Soup

5 large Vidalia onions, sliced thin
2 tablespoons olive oil
1 tablespoon minced garlic
1 teaspoon ground ginger
1 teaspoon dried thyme leaves
4 cups water
1 can vegetable stock
⅔ cup soy sauce

¼ cup balsamic vinegar
½ cup steak sauce
1 tablespoon sugar
½ tablespoon black pepper
⅓ cup red wine
Croutons, optional
Fresh parsley, optional

In a nonstick skillet, brown onions in olive oil with garlic, ginger and thyme until golden brown. Add to a large pot with water, vegetable stock, soy sauce, balsamic vinegar, steak sauce, sugar and black pepper. Bring to a boil; reduce heat to low and cook 20 minutes. Cover and cook 10 more minutes. Before serving, stir in red wine and cook a few more minutes. Serve hot with croutons and garnished with fresh parsley.

Vidalia Onion Beef and Barley Soup

2 pounds lean stew beef, small cubed
1 large Vidalia onion, chopped
Olive oil
1 bell pepper, finely chopped
2 stalks celery, chopped
3 carrots, chopped
½ cup minced cabbage

¾ cup barley
1 bay leaf
3 cans beef broth
7 cups water
1 tablespoon parsley
Salt and pepper to taste

Brown meat and onions with a bit of olive oil. Combine everything in a large stockpot and cook over low heat, covered, approximately 2 hours. For a thicker soup, add a spoonful of flour.

Kielbasa & Cabbage Ale Soup

1 pound kielbasa
4 cans brown ale
4 cups chicken stock
½ cup apple cider vinegar
3 large potatoes, peeled and cubed
1 tablespoon Italian seasoning
1 tablespoon salt

1 tablespoon pepper
2 teaspoons minced garlic
1 large Vidalia onion, chopped
½ head cabbage, chopped
1 tablespoon Worcestershire sauce
1 tablespoon hot sauce

Brown kielbasa and slice into small pieces. Combine everything in a stockpot and simmer over medium heat at least 1 hour. Adjust heat and add water if needed. Serve hot with hot French bread or rolls. You can substitute other types of sausage, if desired.

Split Pea & Ham Soup

2 cans chicken broth
3 cups water
1½ cup dried split peas, sorted and rinsed
1 carrot, chopped
1 cup chopped onion
½ cup chopped celery stalks
1 cup finely chopped ham
¼ teaspoon dried marjoram
⅛ teaspoon Worcestershire sauce
1 bay leaf
Salt and pepper to taste

Combine broth, water and peas in a large covered pot; bring to a boil. Boil 10 minutes; reduce heat to medium low and cover. Simmer 45 minutes to 1 hour, stirring every 15 minutes. Add remaining ingredients, cover and cook an additional 30 minutes. Remove bay leaf and serve hot.

Georgia's Favorite Brunswick Stew

2 pounds chicken, cooked and diced
½ teaspoon ground black pepper
1 teaspoon hot sauce, or to taste
2 tablespoons Worcestershire sauce
2 tablespoons onion salt
4 tablespoons bacon drippings
½ cup barbecue sauce
1½ cups ketchup
2 to 3 cups diced potatoes, cooked
3 (15- to 16-ounce) cans cream-style corn
Salt and pepper to taste

Place all ingredients in a stockpot or large saucepan. Cover and simmer until hot and bubbly. Taste before serving and add more salt, pepper and hot sauce as needed.

Brunswick Rockin' Stewbilee

Brunswick • October

Brunkswick Rockin' Stewbilee is celebrated in October at Mary Ross Waterfront Park in downtown Brunswick. The festivities begin with a live concert and continue with a Stew tasting as more than 50 teams vie for the best Brunswick stew. Also throughout the day, a 5K road race, Pooch Parade, Classic Car Show, Children's Activities, Food and Arts and Crafts. Join us for this fun folklife festival, where the folk heritage roots of Georgia Brunswick stew are celebrated, on display, and can be tasted and eaten!

www.brunswickstewbilee.com

Old-Fashioned Beef Stew

12 ounces boneless beef, cubed
1 cup chopped onion
2 cloves garlic, minced
Olive or vegetable oil
3 potatoes, peeled and diced
5 carrots, sliced
1 can whole-kernel corn, drained
1 can beef broth
1 cup water
½ cup milk
½ tablespoon pepper
½ tablespoon salt
1 tablespoon flour
2 tablespoons brewed coffee (optional)

Brown beef, onions and garlic in a little oil; drain on paper towels to remove excess grease. In a large pot, over medium heat, combine with remaining ingredients and cook about 45 minutes. Thin or thicken as you desire. Serve hot with cornbread muffins.

Brunswick Rockin' Stewbilee
Brunswick

Crockpot Stew Stuff

1 small onion, chopped
1 can tomatoes and green chiles
1 can chopped green chiles
2 cans pinto beans
1 can whole-kernel corn
1 package onion soup mix
1 cup chopped celery
1 large zucchini, chopped
½ cup rice
1 pound smoked sausage, chopped small
1 can sliced black olives
1 pound Monterey Jack cheese, cubed
Tortilla chips

Combine all ingredients, except cheese and chips, in a large crockpot; cook on low for at least 4 hours. Pour over cubed cheese and tortilla chips in the bottom of a serving bowl.

Chicken Taco Stew

1 boneless skinless chicken breast, cubed
1 package taco seasoning mix
1 cup water
1 cup cooked white rice
1 can whole kernel corn, drained
1 (15-ounce) can pinto or chili beans, rinsed and drained

In a large skillet, lightly brown chicken. Add taco seasoning and water; simmer 5 to 10 minutes. Add rice, corn and beans; heat completely. Serve with shredded cheese, sour cream and corn chips.

Scott Herpst, Walker County Messenger

Savory Crockpot Ravioli Stew

4 carrots, sliced
1 Vidalia onion, chopped
½ tablespoon minced garlic
2 cans vegetable broth
1 can diced tomatoes, undrained
1 can green chilies, undrained
1 can cannellini beans, rinsed and drained
1 teaspoon basil
1 teaspoon thyme
Salt and pepper to taste
1 (9-ounce) package refrigerated cheese ravioli
Grated Parmesan cheese
Several slices provolone cheese
Parsley for garnish (optional)

In a large crockpot, combine all ingredients except ravioli, Parmesan cheese, and provolone slices. Cover and cook on high 3½ hours. Stir in ravioli, cover and cook about 10 minutes or until ravioli are tender. Serve in bowls. Sprinkle each bowl with a small amount of Parmesan cheese. Place a slice of provolone cheese gently over each bowl. Top cheese slice with a few parsley sprigs. Serve hot.

Stump On Sports Turkey Chili

1 pound ground turkey
1½ tablespoons olive oil
1 tablespoon kosher salt
1 green bell pepper, seeded and chopped
1 red bell pepper, seeded and chopped
1 jalapeño pepper, seeded and minced
2 cans black beans, undrained
1 can pinto beans, undrained
1 can kidney beans, undrained
1 (20-ounce) can tomato sauce
1 cup water
2 tablespoons chili powder
1 tablespoon garlic powder
1 tablespoon ground cumin
1 tablespoon allspice
1 tablespoon barbecue rub
Dash cinnamon

Brown turkey in olive oil. Add salt and peppers just before meat is completely browned. Drain and place in a large stockpot. Add beans, tomato sauce and water; stir and bring to a near boil. Add remaining spices 1 at a time, stirring them in completely before adding the next. Reduce heat, cover pot and simmer 4 to 5 hours. For best results, make chili a day ahead of time and leave it overnight in the refrigerator. Then reheat it the next day. Serve with cornbread or crackers, sour cream and shredded cheese.

Scott Herpst
Walker County Messenger

Great Miller Lite Chili Cook-Off
Stone Mountain Park • September

The Great Miller Lite Chili Cook-Off festivities include a chili competition, chili samples and live music. Proceeds from the event benefit Camp Twin Lakes, a camp for children with serious illnesses and life challenges. Tickets for adults are $10. Children 12 and under are admitted for free. More than 300 cook-off teams compete in three food categories: chili, Brunswick stew and cornbread. Festival attendees enjoy food samples, live music, and more.

(678) 309-4285 • www.theatlantachilicookoff.com

Falcons Tailgate Beer Chili

2 pounds ground beef
½ pound chopped smoked sausage
2 cans tomato sauce
1 cup salsa
2 cans pinto beans
3 tablespoons chili powder
2 tablespoons Italian seasoning
½ tablespoon minced garlic
1 tablespoon hot sauce
1 can beer
1 chopped onion
1 chopped bell pepper

Brown ground beef in a skillet; drain and pour into large covered pot. Brown sausage in same skillet. Add to pot with remaining ingredients; simmer 2 hours over low heat. Take to the game, heat and enjoy!

Hot Chili Bean Soup with Crispy Tortillas

1 medium onion, sliced
2 tablespoons butter
1 can chili
1 can kidney beans
1 can tomatoes
1 can chopped green chilies
1 jalapeño pepper, minced
1 tablespoon chili powder
1 tablespoon hot sauce
½ teaspoon garlic powder
1 cup shredded Monterey Jack cheese
Corn tortillas
Butter, melted

Combine all ingredients—except cheese, corn tortilla shells, and melted butter—in a large pot; cook over medium heat for 30 minutes. Brush tortilla shells with a very small amount of butter; bake at 350° until crisp. Serve soup topped with cheese and a whole tortilla on the side.

Baked Broccoli Chowder & French Bread

Chowder

2 cups broccoli, crumbled
1 can condensed clam or seafood chowder
½ cup sour cream
¼ cup milk
½ cup shredded Cheddar cheese
½ small onion, chopped
Black pepper

Topping

½ cup shredded Cheddar cheese
Bacon bits
1 can fried onions

Combine chowder ingredients in a baking dish coated with nonstick spray. Bake 25 to 30 minutes at 350°. Sprinkle topping ingredients on top; return to oven until cheese is melted. Serve hot with slices of toasted and buttered French Bread.

Georgia

Vegetables & Other Side Dishes

Cast-Iron Skillet Cheese Potatoes

6 to 7 medium red potatoes
6 tablespoons butter
1½ cups shredded Cheddar cheese
1 small Vidalia onion, minced
Salt and pepper to taste
Dash red pepper flakes, optional
1 can evaporated milk

Clean, peel and slice potatoes. Melt butter in a bowl. In a 12-inch iron skillet or any oven-safe pan, layer ⅓ potato slices. Pour on ⅓ of the butter and cover with ⅓ of the cheese, ⅓ of the onion, and salt and pepper to taste. Repeat layers until finished. Add a dash of red pepper, if desired. Gently pour evaporated milk over all. Bake in a 400° oven 30 to 40 minutes or until potatoes are brown on top.

Creamy Ranch Potatoes

2 pounds small red potatoes
1 (8-ounce) package cream cheese, softened
1 envelope dry buttermilk ranch salad dressing mix
1 can cream of potato soup
Milk as needed

Clean and cube potatoes. In a small bowl, combine cream cheese and salad dressing mix. Stir in soup then potatoes. Cook in a nonstick, covered pot on the stove over medium heat for about 30 minutes, adding milk as needed. Serve when potatoes are soft but not mashed. You can also cook this recipe in the oven or even in a crockpot.

Cheesy Hash Brown Bake

1 can cream of chicken soup
1½ cups milk
½ cup beef broth
2 tablespoons butter, melted
1 teaspoon minced garlic
1½ teaspoon salt
½ teaspoon ground black pepper
1 (30-ounce) package frozen shredded hash browns, thawed
1 cup shredded Colby Jack cheese
5 ounces shredded Swiss cheese

Preheat oven to 350°. In a large bowl, combine soup, milk, broth, butter, garlic, salt and pepper. Fold in hash browns and cheeses until mixed well. Pour into a lightly greased 9x13-inch baking dish. Bake 1 hour or until golden brown.

Scott Herpst
Walker County Messenger

Homemade Scalloped Potatoes

6 to 7 potatoes, thinly sliced
1 can Cheddar cheese soup
1½ cups shredded Cheddar cheese
1 can evaporated milk
1 teaspoon minced onion
Salt and pepper to taste

Combine all ingredients in a covered oven-safe dish and bake at 350° until potatoes are tender.

Sunday Baked Sweet Taters

Casserole

3 cups sweet potatoes, cooked and mashed
1 cup sugar
2 eggs, beaten
1 teaspoon vanilla extract
Pinch of salt
⅓ cup butter

Topping

⅓ cup flour
1 cup brown sugar
1 cup flaked coconut
1 cup chopped pecans
⅓ cup butter, melted

Combine casserole ingredients until smooth. Pour into a 2-quart dish. Mix all topping ingredients and spread over sweet potato mixture. Bake at 350° for 35 to 40 minutes.

Sweet Potato Festival

Ocilla • October

For more than 45 years, the Georgia Sweet Potato Festival has celebrated the beloved Georgia sweet potato. In conjunction with the Riverbend Bluegrass Festival and Annual Motorcycle Rally, there is something for everyone including a Sweet Potato Queen Pageant, cooking contest, parade, arts and crafts, live music, and much more. Visit our festival for family-oriented fun for people of all ages.

229.468.9114

French Fried Sweet Potatoes

3 to 4 sweet potatoes
Oil for frying
Salt

Wash sweet potatoes, cut into thin, French-fry-style slices and dry with paper towels. (Do not cut too thick.) Fry 2 to 3 minutes or until crisp and golden brown. Sprinkle with salt and serve hot. You can also sprinkle with brown sugar, Cajun seasoning or other desired spices.

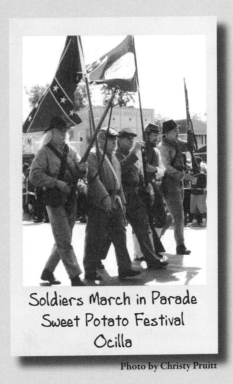

Soldiers March in Parade
Sweet Potato Festival
Ocilla

Photo by Christy Pruitt

Down on the Farm Green Beans

3 strips bacon
½ small onion, thinly sliced
1 (16-ounce) can cut green beans
2 teaspoons cornstarch
¼ teaspoon salt
¼ teaspoon dry mustard
1 tablespoon brown sugar
1 tablespoon vinegar

Cook bacon in large skillet; remove, drain and reserve. Add onions to bacon fat in skillet; cook until clear but not brown. Drain beans, saving ½ cup liquid. Add liquid, cornstarch, salt, mustard, brown sugar and vinegar to skillet. Cook over medium heat, stirring frequently, until mixture boils. Add beans and continue to cook until beans are heated. Serve with reserved bacon crumbled on top. Serves 4.

Snap Beans

1 ham bone, cooked
2 pounds snap beans (aka string beans, green beans)
1 teaspoon sugar
A few hot red pepper flakes
Salt to taste

Place ham bone in pot and add water to cover; bring to a boil. String the beans and snap or cut into desired lengths; add to pot along with sugar and pepper flakes. Cook over medium heat for 1 hour. Season to taste with salt.

Country-Style Baked Beans

2 cans pork 'n beans
1 medium Vidalia onion, diced
6 slices bacon, cooked and crumbled
¾ cup packed brown sugar
½ cup ketchup
¼ cup maple syrup
¼ cup mustard
1 tablespoon vinegar
½ teaspoon mustard
Salt and pepper to taste
⅛ cup Worcestershire sauce
6 slices bacon, uncooked

Combine all ingredients, except raw bacon, in a large bowl; mix well. Pour into a large baking dish and place the 6 slices bacon on top. Bake, uncovered, at 325° at least 1 hour.

Note: You can also add browned ground beef and sausage, if desired.

Fried Farm-Fresh Corn

6 to 8 ears fresh corn, shucked and silks removed
5 tablespoons bacon drippings
1 teaspoon sugar
Salt and pepper
1 cup water

Cut just the tips of the kernels from corn; scrape cob with edge of knife to remove milky portion. Heat bacon drippings (or 5 tablespoons butter) in large skillet over medium heat. Add corn, sugar and salt and pepper to taste. Stir in 1 cup water and continue to cook over medium heat, stirring constantly, until heated through. Lower heat and simmer, stirring frequently (very important as corn is easy to stick and burn), 15 to 20 minutes or until thick. More water should be added as needed.

Fried Corn

2 cans whole-kernel corn, drained
2 tablespoons butter
⅓ cup diced Vidalia onion
1½ teaspoons soy sauce
⅓ cup chopped red bell pepper
⅓ cup chopped green bell pepper
Salt and pepper to taste

In a large skillet, fry corn in butter until edges are golden brown. Add remaining ingredients and continue to cook until heated through. Serve hot.

Variations: For sweet fried corn, add a dash of sugar. For a twist, add Cajun or other seasonings. For a creamy version, use 1 can whole-kernel corn and 1 can cream-style corn. Serve hot.

Tiff's Cornbread Corn Casserole

1 (8½-ounce) package corn muffin mix
2 (15-ounce) cans cream-style corn
1 egg, beaten
⅓ cup butter
¾ cup sour cream

Combine all ingredients; mix well. Pour into greased 9x13-inch baking pan. Bake at 375° for 35 minutes or until done.

Tiffany Nagem
Atlanta, Georgia

Baked Corn and Broccoli

1 can cream-style corn
2 eggs, beaten
2 teaspoons sugar
2 tablespoons flour
1 teaspoon salt
½ cup shredded Cheddar cheese
½ package frozen chopped broccoli

Preheat oven to 350°. Combine corn, eggs, sugar, flour and salt. Add cheese and broccoli; mix well and pour into an oven-safe dish. Bake at 325° for 45 minutes. Serve hot.

Oven-Roasted Squash & Zucchini

2 medium zucchini, cubed
2 medium yellow squash, cubed
1 large red onion, chopped
1 cup cleaned mushrooms
2 large red bell peppers, diced
2 tablespoons olive oil
1½ teaspoons poultry seasoning
1 teaspoon black pepper
Salt to taste

Combine all ingredients in a large zip-close bag and toss to coat evenly. Spread on a nonstick cookie sheet and bake in the oven at 425° until edges brown. Turn once during cooking to allow all sides to cook evenly. Serve hot with seasoned rice.

Summer Flavors Festival
Atlanta • June

The Summer Flavors Festival will serve up flavors from some of Atlanta's best chefs with a slant on very tasty health-conscious foods. Entertainment featured will be the music of renowned pop, R&B, and jazz artists from Atlanta and around the country. Additionally, the festival will promote healthy lifestyles and will be a fundraiser for the TCMS Community Assistant Program, which will benefit the Grady Diabetes Detection and Control Center, as well as cancer organizations.

770.944.7005 • www.summerflavors.com

Fried Okra

1 pound fresh okra
2 eggs, beaten
½ tablespoon hot sauce
1 cup cornmeal
1 tablespoon flour
½ teaspoon salt
½ teaspoon cayenne pepper
Hot oil

Wash okra and drain. Cut off and discard ends; slice okra into thin pieces. In a bowl, combine beaten eggs and hot sauce. Stir in okra and mix until well coated. In a shallow dish, combine cornmeal, flour, salt and cayenne. Combine all and toss to coat evenly. Fry in hot oil until golden brown. Drain on a paper towel for about 30 seconds; serve hot.

Collard Greens

1 ham hock
4 quarts water
5 pounds collard greens, washed and stems removed
1 tablespoon sugar
1 tablespoon hot sauce
Salt and pepper

Place water and ham hock in a large pan and bring to a boil. Reduce heat, cover and cook about 1 hour. Wash collard greens again and cut in half; add to pot with sugar and hot sauce. Cover, reduce heat, and simmer over medium heat about 2 hours. Season to taste with salt and pepper. Serve hot.

Baked Asparagus

1 pound asparagus
1 tablespoon olive oil
Salt and pepper
1 lemon
2 tablespoons sesame seeds

Rinse and dry asparagus; trim ends of stalks and place in baking pan. Drizzle with olive oil; add a few dashes of salt and pepper. Spritz with juice of 1 lemon and top with sesame seeds. Bake at 375° until tender, about 10 minutes.

Stewed Cabbage & Beef

1 small head cabbage
½ pound ground beef
1 can diced tomatoes, undrained
1 can green chilies, undrained
1 medium Vidalia onion, chopped
1 can whole-kernel corn, undrained
1 teaspoon garlic salt
½ cup chopped celery
1 can ranch-style beans
1 tablespoon chili powder
Salt and pepper to taste
⅔ cup water

Delicious as a side, soup, stew or even a main dish.

Slice cabbage into thin slices. Brown ground beef; drain. Mix all ingredients in a stockpot or crockpot. When cooking on the stove, cook on medium covered until cabbage is soft. When using a crockpot, cook on high, covered, until cabbage is soft.

Georgia

Mac's Ultimate Mac and Cheese

1 box penne pasta
2 to 3 tablespoons olive oil
1 garlic clove, minced
¼ cup white wine
⅔ cup heavy cream
¾ cup shredded mozzarella cheese
¼ cup chopped smoked Gouda cheese
¼ cup grated Parmesan cheese

Cook pasta per directions on box; drain. In a large pan over medium-high heat, combine olive oil and garlic; cook until garlic is soft. Add wine and reduce while stirring. Stir in cream, cheeses and noodles. Continue to stir until noodles are covered with melted cheese.

Chef Mac Griffith, born in Lakeview, Georgia

Author Kent Whitaker and wife Ally
North Georgia Mountains

Fried Green Tomatoes

3 green tomatoes
1 ½ cups buttermilk
2 eggs, lightly beaten
1 tablespoon plus 1 ½ cups self-rising flour, divided
Salt and pepper
2 cups vegetable oil

Wash tomatoes and slice thin. Combine buttermilk, egg, 1 tablespoon four and salt and pepper to taste. Add tomato slices; set aside. Heat oil to 350 degrees in a heavy skillet. While oil is heating, combine remaining four with salt and pepper to taste. Remove one tomato slice from buttermilk mixture; toss in flour mixture, coating thoroughly. Place in heated oil and fry until golden brown. Repeat with remaining tomato slices. You can cook more than one tomato slice at a time being careful to leave plenty of room so slices do not touch or overlap. Drain on paper towels and serve immediately. Serves 6.

Georgia Peach Pasta Salad

6 ounces penne pasta
2 tablespoons olive oil
2 cups chopped fresh spinach
½ zucchini, cut in strips
4 fresh peaches, peeled and chopped
⅓ cup grated Parmesan cheese
2 tablespoons basil
2 tablespoons white vinegar
½ teaspoon ground black pepper

Boil pasta until tender; drain. Heat olive oil in skillet. Add spinach and zucchini; sauté until limp. Toss with pasta, peaches, cheese, basil, vinegar and pepper in salad bowl. Toss thoroughly to blend ingredients. Makes 8 servings.

Pork

Fried Maple Pork Chops

8 (¾-inch thick) pork chops
Maple Syrup
Black pepper
Paprika
All-purpose flour
Minced onion

Spread a very small amount of maple syrup over each pork chop. Sprinkle with salt, black pepper and paprika. Dredge lightly in flour and fry in a hot nonstick skillet using a small amount of oil. While cooking, add minced onion. Serve hot. You can substitute your favorite sauce, such as soy sauce or barbecue sauce for the maple syrup, if desired.

Syrup Making & Storytelling Festival

Jarrell Plantation, Juliette • November

Syrup making was an important fall event on middle Georgia farms. Jarrell Plantation Park's Syrup Makin' & Storytelling Festival brings the event back to life with demonstrations of the sugar cane mill, syrup kettle, steam engine, woodstove cooking and storytelling.

478.986.5172

Country Fried Pork Chops

6 to 8 pork chops
2 tablespoons Worcestershire sauce
⅔ cup flour
½ cup cornmeal
½ teaspoon salt
½ teaspoon black pepper
1 large egg, beaten
2 tablespoons milk
Oil

Coat pork chops in a light coating of Worcestershire sauce. In a bowl, combine flour, cornmeal, flour, salt and pepper. In another bowl, combine egg and milk. Dunk pork chops in egg mixture then dredge in flour mixture. Cook in a hot skillet with oil until golden brown; serve hot.

Syrup Makin' Festival at Jarrell Plantation
Juliette, Georgia

Vidalia Orange Pork Chops

4 to 6 pork chops
½ cup minced Vidalia onion
½ cup orange juice
2 tablespoons olive oil
2 garlic cloves, crushed
2 teaspoons ground cumin
¼ teaspoon coarsely ground black pepper

Preparing this recipe is a snap!

Combine all ingredients in a large zip-close bag or covered bowl; refrigerate at least 1 hour or longer (overnight if possible) ensuring all chops are well coated. Remove and grill or bake. Serve hot with fresh veggies.

North Georgia Apple Pork Chops

6 boneless pork chops
½ teaspoon coarsely ground black pepper
½ teaspoon cumin powder
1 teaspoon vegetable oil
¼ cup apple juice
2 tablespoons apple jelly
2 tablespoons Dijon mustard
1 North Georgia apple, finely chopped

You can use any apple with this recipe, but make it with an apple from the mountains of North Georgia if at all possible.

Season chops with pepper and cumin powder. In a large nonstick skillet, over medium-high heat, brown chops in a small amount of oil on 1 side. Stir in apple juice, jelly and mustard. Coat each chop and stir in apples. Continue to cook until chops are done. Serve hot.

Oven Baked Country-Style Ribs

4 pounds country-style ribs
½ cup cider vinegar
2 tablespoons soy sauce
1 teaspoon salt
Dash cayenne pepper
1 can tomato soup
½ cup brown sugar
1 teaspoon celery seed
1 teaspoon chili powder

Combine all ingredients in a large oven-safe dish. Cook, covered, in a 350° oven about 45 minutes. Stir ribs to coat evenly. Cover and continue to bake about 15 minutes. Uncover and cook another 5 to 10 minutes before removing from oven. Serve hot.

Amicalola Falls
Dawsonville

Crockpot Pulled Pork Barbecue

1 pork roast
1 tablespoon lemon juice
1 small onion, chopped
1 tablespoon brown sugar
¼ cup minced Vidalia onion
1 bottle barbecue sauce
1 tablespoon soy sauce
1 tablespoon apple cider vinegar
1 cup water

Combine everything, except water, in a large crockpot. Add about ½ cup water, cover and cook on high about 3 hours. Depending on your crockpot and how many times you open the lid, you may need to add the rest of the water, but most likely not. As roast cooks, you will be able to shred with a fork. When completely shredded, cook an additional 30 minutes. Serve hot. Cooking time can vary from 3 to 5 hours depending on your crockpot and the size of the roast.

Big Pig Jig
Vienna • October

BIG PIG JIG® was born when a group of self-professed gourmets bet who among them could cook the most succulent pig! That year, 1982, the barbecue competition combined with a well-attended arts and crafts fair and the county's annual hog show. The festival has now expanded to include other barbecue cooking contests, a parade, sidewalk art contest, 5K Hog Jog, QuizFest academic scholarship competition, local, regional, and national entertainment, and more. BIG PIG JIG® remains the southeast's largest and Georgia's oldest and OFFICIAL barbecue cooking contest.

229.268.8275 • www.bigpigjig.com

Georgia

Grilled BBQ Pork Chop Sandwich

1 pound thin-sliced pork chops
1 cup barbecue sauce
1 green bell pepper, sliced
1 yellow ell pepper, sliced
1 small Vidalia onion, sliced
Hamburger Buns

In a bowl, combine pork chops and barbecue sauce. Place veggies on aluminum foil. Grill pork chops and veggies to desired doneness and serve hot on buns.

Ramblin' Wreck Pork Tenderloin

1 pork tenderloin
Cajun seasoning
Salt and pepper
Soy sauce
1 can cream of mushroom soup
1 cup water
1 foil pan
Large yeast rolls for buns, warm

I first tried this pork tenderloin sandwich outside of a Georgia Tech football game.

Rub tenderloin with Cajun seasoning, salt and pepper. Drizzle with soy sauce and wrap as tightly as possible in cling wrap. Chill at least 1 hour (overnight if possible). Remove from cling wrap and grill over high heat to sear outside and leave grill marks. In a foil pan, large enough for tenderloin, combine soup and water. Cut tenderloin in half, if needed, and place in pan. Simmer over medium-high heat. When done, slice while still hot and serve on warm yeast rolls.

Honey-Sesame Pork Roast

1 pork roast
2 teaspoons vegetable oil
1 (14½-ounce) can diced tomatoes, undrained
½ cup minced onion
1 garlic clove, crushed
1 teaspoon ground ginger
2 teaspoons ground cinnamon
¼ cup honey
1 tablespoon toasted sesame seeds

Sear all sides of roast in a nonstick skillet with a small amount of oil. Place in a roasting pan; add tomatoes, onion, garlic, ginger, cinnamon and honey. Cover with foil and bake at 375° until juices run clear. Top with sesame seeds before removing from oven.

Barbecued Pork Butt

1 pork shoulder or pork butt
1 tablespoon chili powder
1 tablespoon pepper
½ tablespoon salt
½ cup mustard
½ cup apple cider vinegar

Rinse pork with cool water and remove excess fat, if needed. Combine remaining ingredients in a large bowl. Place pork in bowl and cover evenly. Cover and refrigerate 2 hours or overnight. Smoke pork in smoker using indirect heat and hickory wood at least 2 hours. Remove from smoker, rub with a bit of oil and additional spices, if desired; wrap tightly in foil. Place on a covered grill or in the oven and cook on 350° about 1 to 2 hours depending on size. If cooking in the oven, place foil-wrapped meat in a large pan. Grease will drip from the foil. When done, remove from oven and either slice or pull with a fork. Sprinkle with a bit of pepper and serve hot with your favorite sauce.

Georgia

Italian Pepper Sliced Pork

4 to 5 boneless pork chops
2 to 3 tablespoons olive oil
1 teaspoon butter
2 tablespoons lemon juice
1¼ cups beef broth
1 tablespoon flour
3 green onions, chopped
1 red bell pepper, chopped
2 cloves garlic, minced
½ teaspoon dried thyme
Salt and pepper

Slice pork into strips. Melt butter and olive oil in a nonstick skillet over medium heat. Add lemon juice and beef broth; stir in flour. Add remaining ingredients and cook until pork is done. Remove pork (leave vegetables); add 2 tablespoons water to skillet. When water is browned, pour vegetable mixture over pork. Serve hot over rice or steamed vegetables.

Centennial Park
Atlanta

Ale Marinated Pork Cutlets

4 tenderized (¼-inch thick) pork cutlets
1 bottle dark ale
1 garlic clove, minced
½ cup chopped parsley
¼ cup flour
⅛ cup finely crushed corn chips
½ teaspoon salt
1 teaspoon ground black pepper
2 teaspoons butter
2 tablespoons cider vinegar
2 tablespoons prepared mustard
2 teaspoons brown sugar
2 teaspoons dill weed

Marinate pork in ale with minced garlic and parsley at least 1 hour. Combine flour and crushed corn chips in a shallow plate. Remove chops from ale. Bring half the ale marinade to roiling boil in a small saucepan; boil about five minutes. Dredge each chop in flour mixture for a light coating; sprinkle with salt and pepper. Melt butter in a large skillet over medium-high heat; add breaded cutlets and cook until golden brown on 1 side. Turn cutlets, add remaining ingredients to skillet and continue to cook until pork is cooked through; remove cutlets. Add boiled marinade to skillet and cook with pan juices and until thickened. Serve over pork cutlets.

Georgia

Ginger Pork & Oriental Peanut Sauce

Ginger Pork

Pork chops, thinly sliced (or other thin-sliced pork)
½ cup orange juice
2 tablespoons soy sauce
2 tablespoons ground ginger
1 teaspoon minced garlic
1 teaspoon chili powder
1 teaspoon red wine vinegar
½ teaspoon salt

Oriental Peanut Sauce

½ cup light soy sauce
1 tablespoon creamy peanut butter
¼ cup red wine vinegar
2 teaspoons ground ginger
2 tablespoons brown sugar
1 tablespoon minced onion

Combine Ginger Pork ingredients in a bowl; stir to mix well, cover and chill a few hours. In a separate bowl, combine Oriental Peanut Sauce ingredients; mix until smooth (A few drops of water can be used to thin; additional peanut butter can be used to thicken.) In a skillet, cook pork along with the marinade. Serve hot over rice or noodles with veggies and Oriental Peanut Sauce on the side.

Wiener Schnitzel

4 to 6 (½-inch-thick) pork or veal cutlets
Salt and pepper
1 cup breadcrumbs
2 eggs, beaten
Cooking oil

Pound cutlets to about ¼- or ⅛-thick. Mix salt and pepper into the breadcrumbs. Dip cutlets into crumbs, then into beaten eggs, then back into crumbs. Fry in hot oil, on both sides until golden brown, about 2 to 4 minutes each side. Serve with potato salad, Spaetzle or red cabbage and garnish with a lemon wedge.

Oktoberfest
Helen, Georgia

Oktoberfest
Savannah • October

Savannah's annual Oktoberfest on the River is one of those great fall events that people actually plan their vacations around. The riverfront festival is filled with bratwursts, oompah band music, artists and craftsmen and one of the most popular Wiener Dog Races in the country! There are games for the kids and River Street is filled with world famous restaurants. Get your oompah on at Oktoberfest on the River.

912.234.0295 • www.riverstreetsavannah.com

Georgia

Chopped Pork & Peppers over Rice

3 cups cubed pork
Oil
2 green bell peppers, sliced
½ small Vidalia onion, chopped
⅓ cup flour
1 teaspoon salt
½ teaspoon garlic salt
1 teaspoon mustard
2 tablespoons oil
1 can cream of mushroom soup
4 cups prepared rice

In a skillet, brown cubed pork in a small amount of oil (do not overcook as it will continue to cook in the oven). Combine remaining ingredients in a baking dish, add pork and bake at 350° about 30 minutes. Serve hot over rice.

Pork Taco Wraps

1½ pounds sliced or ground pork (not sausage)
Oil
1 cup finely chopped onion
1 teaspoon each minced garlic, cumin, lemon juice and salt
½ teaspoon ground black pepper
1 cup coarsely chopped fresh cilantro
Flour tortillas, shredded lettuce, tomatoes, sour cream, etc.

Brown pork in a large skillet in a small amount of oil; drain. Add onion and seasonings; continue to cook until pork is fully cooked. Serve hot with flour tortillas, shredded lettuce, tomatoes, sour cream or more.

Mac's Jerk Pork Kabobs

1½ pounds pork loin, cubed
Salt and pepper
4 tablespoons jerk seasoning, divided
⅔ cup olive oil
1 mango, peeled, pitted and cubed
1 can pineapple chunks
1 red onion, peeled and sliced (for kabobs)
2 red bell peppers, sliced (for kabobs)
Hot sauce

Mac has worked in the food industry for years. "It all started with my dad. He was in charge of cooking for officers and thousands of men when he served in the army and could easily feed a few or a huge crowd!"

Coat pork with salt and pepper to taste and 2 tablespoons jerk seasoning. In a skillet over medium heat, brown pork in olive oil and remaining 2 tablespoons jerk seasoning. Stir in fruit and vegetables to brown edges. Remove from heat and alternate ingredients on soaked bamboo skewers. Coat with juices from skillet. When ready, grill to desired doneness. Serve hot with a splash of hot sauce.

Chef Mac Griffith, born in Lakeview, Georgia

Bourbon Pork Kabobs

1 pound boneless pork chops, cubed
2 tablespoons bourbon
4 tablespoons spicy mustard
4 tablespoons brown sugar
2 tablespoons soy sauce
½ tablespoon apple cider vinegar
Sliced vegetables (onion, bell pepper, tomatoes, squash, etc.)

Combine all ingredients, except vegetables, in a covered bowl; chill for an hour. Place cubed pork on skewers with your favorite sliced vegetables. Grill over medium heat or bake in oven at 400°. Serve hot over rice.

Smoked Sausage & Veggies with Spanish Rice

1 pound smoked pork sausage, chopped
1 box Spanish rice
3 cups water
1 small bag stir-fry-style frozen vegetables
⅔ cup Georgia pecan halves (optional)
Tabasco

I prefer sliced smoked sausage for this recipe, but ground sausage will work in a pinch.

Brown sausage slices in a skillet. Combine sausage and remaining ingredients, except Tabasco, in a saucepan. Cook, covered, over medium heat until rice is tender and excess water is gone. Serve hot in a bowl with a few dashes of hot sauce.

Sausage & Potato Dinner

1 pound ground sausage, browned and drained
Oil
4 potatoes, peeled and sliced
1 small onion, diced
1 can Cheddar cheese (or cream of mushroom) soup
⅓ cup water

In a large skillet, brown sausage; drain and set aside. Wipe skillet and cover bottom with a small amount of oil; heat to medium. Add potatoes and onion; cook until browned. Combine soup and water; pour into skillet. Gently stir and cook just until soup is hot and potatoes are tender. Serve hot.

Sausage Mac

½ pound pork sausage
½ cup chopped onion
1 small green bell pepper, chopped
1 can diced tomatoes, drained
1 cup sour cream
⅓ cup milk
1½ cups elbow macaroni
1 teaspoon sugar
1½ teaspoons chili powder
½ teaspoon salt
2 slices cheese

In a large nonstick skillet, brown sausage; drain. Stir in onions, bell peppers and diced tomatoes. Add sour cream, milk, macaroni, sugar, chili powder and salt. Cover and simmer, stirring occasionally, about 15 minutes or until noodles are cooked. Add additional milk or a bit of water, if needed. Before serving, remove from heat and stir in cheese until melted. Serve hot.

Sweet & Spicy Grilled Ham Steak

2 to 4 bone-in ham steaks
Black pepper
⅔ cup ketchup
⅓ cup sweet pickle relish
1 tablespoon soy sauce
1 tablespoon hot sauce
1 tablespoon cider vinegar
1 teaspoon brown sugar

Sprinkle each ham steak with a small amount of black pepper. Combine remaining ingredients in a bowl to make a sauce. (Double if needed for additional steaks.) Baste each steak evenly with sauce and grill over medium-high heat 3 to 4 minutes on each side depending on thickness of steak. Turn and baste as needed. Serve hot.

Country Ham & Easy Red Eye Gravy

Country ham slices, ¼-inch-thick
Pepper
Butter
Brown sugar
Prepared coffee

Cook ham slices in a hot skillet for a few minutes each side. Depending on the fat, do NOT trim, you may need to add some butter. Chances are the ham is already pretty salty so just sprinkle with a bit of pepper. When ham is cooked, remove to a plate. To make gravy, keep all bits and pieces along with ham grease and butter in the skillet. Add water by the spoonful to make a sauce. Sprinkle with a bit of brown sugar and a few drops of coffee. Serve ham hot over biscuits with a spoonful of gravy over the top.

Cola Baked Ham

1 picnic ham
3 cans cola
½ cup brown sugar
Water
1 large can pineapple slices

Combine cola and sugar in a large stockpot. Add ham then water to cover. Cook over low heat, covered, about 2 hours. If needed, very carefully remove ham and flip it. (I have found that taking the stockpot outside, using some tongs, large forks and helping hands from a friend makes this much easier.) After about three hours of low cooking, transfer ham to a deep pan. Baste with cooking juice and add some to cover bottom of pan. Secure pineapple to ham using toothpicks. Pour remaining pineapple juice into pan. Bake in a 350° oven, basting occasionally, for about 30 minutes.

Tybee Island Lighthouse
Tybee Island

Georgia

Vidalia Onion & Ham Bruschetta

½ pound thin-sliced deli ham
1 cup chopped Vidalia onion
1 cup chopped tomatoes
2 tablespoons mayonnaise
1 tablespoon Dijon mustard
Sliced Italian bread
Salt and pepper
Italian Seasoning
Sliced mozzarella cheese

Combine ham, onion, tomatoes, mayonnaise and mustard in a bowl. Arrange bread on a large baking sheet. Top with ham mixture, a few dashes of salt, pepper and Italian seasoning, and a slice of mozzarella. Bake at 350° about 10 minutes. Serve hot and open faced.

Smoked Ham Monte Cristo

½ pound thin-sliced deli smoked ham
Swiss cheese, sliced
1 loaf French bread, sliced
Salt and pepper
3 eggs, beaten
⅓ cup milk
3 tablespoons butter

For each sandwich, place equal amounts ham and 2 slices cheese between 2 slices French bread. Add a dash of salt and pepper. In a small bowl, combine eggs and milk. Carefully dip each sandwich in egg mixture (stir together more milk and eggs, if needed). Melt butter in a large skillet and cook each sandwich until eggs are cooked and cheese is melted. Serve hot.

Wrapped BLT with Garlic Mayo

1 to 2 pounds cooked bacon
6 (10-inch) flour tortillas
6 tablespoons mayonnaise
1 teaspoon minced garlic
Shredded lettuce
Sliced tomatoes
Salt and pepper

Cook bacon and drain on a paper towel. Combine mayonnaise and garlic in a small bowl. Coat tortilla with Garlic Mayo then layer on lettuce and tomato; season with salt and pepper. Roll up and serve.

Georgia

Beef

Hot Burgers

2 pounds ground beef
1 packet chili seasoning
1 packet taco seasoning
1 tablespoon minced jalapeño pepper
Pepper cheese

Combine everything except cheese in a bowl. Form into hamburger patties and grill; top with pepper cheese. For meatloaf, add an egg and 1 cup crushed tortilla chips and bake at 350° until done.

Crockpot Baked Beef and Beans

1 pound ground beef
1 small Vidalia onion, chopped
1 green bell pepper, chopped
2 cans pork & beans
1 can black beans, drained
¾ cup brown sugar
2 tablespoons prepared mustard
2 tablespoons Worcestershire sauce
2 cups ketchup
½ tablespoon cumin powder

Brown beef in skillet; drain. Add to crockpot with remaining ingredients. Cook on high 3 hours stirring occasionally.

Georgia

Pot Luck

1 pound ground beef
1 large cabbage
3 medium potatoes, sliced
1 large onion
Salt and pepper

Brown ground beef. In a separate pot, steam cabbage, potatoes and onion in 1 cup water until tender. Add hamburger to cabbage; salt and pepper to taste. Simmer 15 minutes and enjoy.

Melba Sorrell Locher
Hahira, Georgia

Susan's Beefy Ranch Goulash

1 pound ground beef
4 to 5 potatoes, peeled and cubed
½ tablespoon garlic powder
½ tablespoon salt
½ tablespoon black pepper
2 cans cream of mushroom soup
1 cup shredded Cheddar cheese
Ranch dressing

Brown ground beef; drain. Boil cubed potatoes until tender; drain. Combine beef, potatoes, garlic, salt, pepper and cream of mushroom soup in a large greased baking dish. Bake at 350° about 20 minutes. Remove from oven, top with cheese, return to oven long enough for cheese to melt. Serve hot with a small amount of ranch dressing drizzled over each serving.

Susan Bowman
Ringgold, Georgia

Enchilada Casserole

1 pound ground beef
1 chili seasoning packet
1 large bag plain tortilla chips
2 cups shredded cheese, divided
1 jar enchilada or taco sauce
1 can tomato sauce
⅓ cup diced onions
⅓ cup diced bell pepper
½ cup sour cream

Brown and drain ground beef; combine with chili pack. Add a few spoonfuls of water to mix well. Spread ⅓ bag tortilla chips in the bottom of a casserole dish. Sprinkle about ¾ cup cheese over tortilla chips. Cover with half of ground beef and sauces. Make another layer of ⅓ bag tortilla chips, ¾ cup cheese, beef and sauces. Top with onions and bell pepper. Bake in a 375° oven, uncovered, for 30 minutes. Spread top of casserole with sour cream and cover with remaining ½ cup cheese. Bake until cheese is melted.

Fiesta Atlanta
Atlanta • May

Atlanta's largest Hispanic outdoor family festival, Fiesta Atlanta takes place in May at Centennial Olympic Park in downtown Atlanta. More than 30,000 people attend Atlanta's annual signature Hispanic event. Fiesta Atlanta takes place on Cinco de Mayo weekend; it is a day long celebration of Latino culture, music, and food. Fiesta Atlanta features continuous live performances by national and local artists, vendor booths offering free product samples, arts and crafts, and authentic Latino foods. It is a free event.

404.350.0200 • www.fiestaatlanta.com

South of the Border
Beef 'n Cornbread Casserole

1 pound ground beef
¼ cup water
3 tablespoon margarine
2¼ cups cornbread stuffing mix
1 egg, slightly beaten
1 can chili with beans
1 small can chili peppers
1½ cups shredded Pepper Jack cheese, divided

Talk about stick to your ribs...
this casserole is hearty and filling.
It's perfect for dinners and potluck events.

Brown and drain ground beef; set aside. Combine water and margarine in a large saucepan and heat until butter melts. Turn off heat and add in stuffing mix and egg until well blended. Coat a 2-quart baking dish with nonstick spray; press stuffing mixture firmly over bottom of dish to make a crust. In a large bowl, combine beef, chili, peppers and 1 cup cheese. Pour mixture into crust and cook at 400° for 30 minutes. Top with remaining ½ cup cheese and cook until melted. Serve hot.

Bulldog Casserole

1 pound ground beef
1 medium onion, chopped
¼ green bell pepper, chopped
1 (16-ounce) can chopped tomatoes
1 tablespoon ketchup
1 tablespoon A1 sauce
1 tablespoon Worcestershire sauce
1 (5-ounce) package elbow macaroni
1 can cream of chicken soup
Salt and pepper
2 cups shredded Cheddar cheese

Mix this delicious, easy casserole in disposable metal pans and keep them in the freezer to cook for the game.

Preheat oven to 350°. In a large skillet, brown beef with onions; drain. Add bell pepper, tomatoes, ketchup, A1 and Worcestershire. Simmer 20 to 30 minutes. Cook macaroni in salted boiling water until almost soft; drain. Combine meat mixture, macaroni, soup and salt and pepper to taste in a 9x13-inch glass baking dish. Cover with cheese and bake 20 minutes or until heated through and cheese is melted.

Hamburger Steak 'n Gravy Dinner

1½ pounds ground beef
1 teaspoon garlic powder
1 pack onion soup mix
1 small Vidalia onion, sliced
1 package brown gravy mix
1 small can mushrooms

In a bowl, combine ground beef, garlic powder and soup mix. Mix well and form into large patties. In a skillet, brown patties but do not fully cook. Place browned patties in a casserole dish and cover with onions. (You can also add green bell peppers, if desired.) Prepare gravy according to package directions; pour over top of patties and cover with mushrooms. Bake at 350° about 20 minutes. Delicious with hot rolls and mashed potatoes.

Cheryl's Beefy Polish Mistakes

2 pounds ground chuck
1 pound hot pork sausage
1 medium onion, chopped
½ teaspoon garlic powder plus more for rolls
¼ teaspoon oregano
¼ teaspoon Worcestershire sauce
1 pound Velveeta cheese
1 package small hoagie or sour dough rolls
4 tablespoons margarine, melted

Joe was born in Warner Robins, Georgia, home of the 2007 Little League World Series Champions.

Brown ground beef, sausage and onion; drain. Add seasonings and cheese. Cook over low heat until cheese is melted. Remove center of rolls and stuff with meat mixture. Brush rolls with margarine and sprinkle with garlic powder. Bake at 350° 15 to 20 minutes. These "Mistakes" can be made in advance and frozen before baking, a quick and easy snack for an after school pick-me-up for the kids.

Joe and Cheryl Norman

Crockpot Sloppy Joes

2 pounds ground beef
¼ cup finely chopped celery
½ Vidalia onion, chopped
2 tablespoons flour
1 cup water
1 cup ketchup
1 cup tomato sauce
2 teaspoons apple cider vinegar
¼ cup brown sugar
1 teaspoon chili powder
1 small bell pepper, minced
1½ tablespoons Worcestershire sauce

In a skillet, brown meat; drain. Combine browned meat and remaining ingredients in a crockpot and cook on high 4 to 5 hours.

Kid's Chili Pie Cups

1½ pounds ground beef
1 onion, chopped
1 can chili
¼ teaspoon pepper
1 package chili seasoning
Corn chips
1 cup shredded Cheddar cheese
Fat free sour cream

A very simple recipe best made with the help of little hands.

In a skillet, brown beef and onion; drain. Stir in chili, pepper and chili seasoning. Use foil-style cup cake liners and a muffin tin. Let the kids layer the chips, meat filling, and cheese in the cups. Bake until cheese melts or serve as the cups are filled with no baking. This also works great in coffee mugs! Top with a bit of sour cream before serving.

Sunday Family Meatloaf

4 tablespoons butter
1 Vidalia onion, chopped
1 stalk celery, finely chopped
1 green bell pepper, chopped
1 teaspoon paprika
1 teaspoon black pepper
1 tablespoon Worcestershire sauce
1 tablespoon steak sauce
⅓ cup milk
½ cup ketchup
2 pounds ground beef
½ pound ground pork sausage
2 eggs, beaten
1 cup breadcrumbs
2 teaspoons minced garlic
2 teaspoons brown sugar
1 can tomato sauce
Garlic powder to taste
Mushroom, olives, salsa, brown gravy, or ketchup for topping

Melt butter in a large saucepan over medium heat with onion, celery, bell pepper, paprika, black pepper, Worcestershire sauce and steak sauce. Cook 5 to 10 minutes to reduce liquid. Reduce heat to low and scrape bottom of pan to loosen any stuck particles. Stir in milk and ketchup until well blended; remove from heat to cool. In a large bowl, combine beef, sausage, eggs and remaining ingredients except topping. Add cooled onion mixture. Place in a large baking dish; bake at 350° about 45 minutes. Before removing from oven, top with your choice of mushrooms, olives, salsa, a brown gravy mix packet or just plain ketchup.

Barbecue Beef Meatloaf

½ pound finely chopped or
   shredded smoked barbecue beef
1 pound ground beef
1 cup breadcrumbs
2 eggs, beaten
½ cup chopped onion
¼ teaspoon salt
¼ teaspoon pepper
¼ cup barbecue sauce

Combine ingredients in a large bowl and mix well. Place into a loaf pan and cook at 350° for 45 to 50 minutes. Remove from oven, top with a small amount of barbecue sauce and cook another 15 minutes or until done.

Georgia folks know barbecue. Here is a delicious way to add some barbecue flavor to your next meatloaf.

Simply Southern Jubilee
Hampton • April

Enjoy all things Southern! The Simply Southern Jubilee includes a Memphis Barbecue Network sanctioned cook-off, bluegrass music, living history exhibit and reenactment (battle 2:00 pm each day), arts and crafts, a children's area, good food and much more!

770.957.5786
www.simplysouthernjubilee.com

Seasoned Grilled Steaks with Italian Butter

3 to 4 steaks (your choice)
Italian dressing
Salt and pepper

Marinate steaks 1 hour in a light coating of Italian dressing. Sprinkle with salt and pepper to taste. Cook steaks on the grill, in the oven or on the stove to your desired doneness. Top with Italian Butter.

Italian Butter

⅓ cup butter, softened
Italian seasoning
Dash sugar
Pinch minced garlic
A few drops olive oil, if desired
Large dash parsley

Combine butter and remaining ingredients to taste; mix well. Chill; serve over hot steaks.

Simply Southern Jubilee
Hampton, Georgia

Provided by Henry County Parks & Recreation

Salsa Covered Grilled Ribeye

4 ribeye steaks
½ tablespoon chili powder
½ tablespoon onion powder
½ tablespoon cumin
1 to 2 tablespoons chopped parsley
½ tablespoon cilantro, optional
Salt and pepper to taste
1 tablespoon water
Chunky salsa

Combine chili powder, onion powder, cumin, parsley, cilantro, salt and pepper to taste, and water to create a thick, moist rub. Spread evenly over each steak. Grill steaks to preferred doneness. Warm salsa slightly in microwave. Serve steaks hot with a few spoonfuls of heated salsa on top.

Wes Spencer, born in Athens, Georgia

Chickamauga National Battlefield
Fort Oglethorpe

Jeff Kinsey • shutterstock.com

Georgia

Mini Vidalia Onion Beef Wellington

6 to 8 center-cut fillet mignon
Salt and freshly ground black pepper
2 tablespoons vegetable oil
1 can chopped mushrooms (or fresh)
2 tablespoons butter
1 small Vidalia onion, chopped
2 tablespoons minced garlic
2 eggs
2 puff pastry sheets

The key to this easy and delicious Beef Welligton is searing the edges of the meat but not over cooking it before wrapping with pastry shell. Give it a try!

Season meat with salt and pepper and sear on both sides in hot oil. Do not fully cook, only sear the outsides. Remove meat from skillet then add mushrooms, butter, onion, garlic and salt and pepper to taste. Cook until warmed through, remove from heat and set aside. In a small bowl, lightly beat eggs to make an egg wash. Roll out pastry and cut evenly to fully wrap each serving. In the middle of each pastry, place equal amounts mushroom mixture and top with a serving of meat. Gently wrap corners using egg wash to seal edges; brush with egg wash. Cook at 425° on a nonstick pan until pastry is golden brown. Serve hot.

Steak on a Shingle

½ pound thinly sliced steak (or chipped beef)
Olive oil
1 tablespoon steak sauce
¼ teaspoon salt
¼ teaspoon pepper
5 tablespoons all-purpose flour
1 cup milk
1 cup water
1 teaspoon sugar
Texas Toast
Butter
Garlic powder

In a skillet, brown steak in small amount of olive oil until slightly brown; stir in steak sauce, salt and pepper. Add flour, milk, water and sugar. Stir over low heat until gravy thickens. Serve hot over buttered Texas toast with a bit of garlic powder.

Country Fried Steak

2 pounds bottom or top round steak
½ cup jelly or jam (any flavor you prefer)
2 tablespoons Worcestershire sauce
⅔ cup flour
¼ cup cornmeal
½ teaspoon salt
½ teaspoon black pepper
1 large egg
2 tablespoons water
¾ cup buttermilk baking mix (such as Bisquick)
⅓ cup vegetable oil

Cut steaks into equal portions and pound to desired thickness. Combine jelly and Worcestershire in a bowl; marinate steaks about 30 minutes. Use a paper towel to wipe off excess marinade. In a shallow plate, sift together flour, cornmeal, salt, and pepper. In another shallow plate, combine egg and water. In still another shallow plate, place baking mix. Coat steaks in flour mixture, dip in egg mixture, and then coat with baking mix. Heat vegetable oil over medium-high heat in a cast-iron skillet (or other large skillet); cook steaks until golden brown. Serve crunchy steaks hot and covered in gravy with potatoes, peas and tea.

Milk Gravy

Flour
Pepper
Milk

Pour excess oil from skillet leaving 2 to 3 tablespoons and drippings. Add a few spoonfuls flour, season with pepper and stir to mix. When hot, but not yet browning, add milk to desired consistency mixing well. Simmer until ready to serve.

Tiff's Salisbury Steak Dinner

1 tablespoon olive oil
2 pounds cubed steak
Salt and pepper
1 (29-ounce) can tomato sauce
1 (14¾-ounce) can beef gravy
1 (28-ounce) package frozen diced potatoes with onions and peppers

Heat olive oil in a skillet over medium heat. Brown steaks in hot oil with black pepper and salt to taste. Drain on paper towels then place in a large stockpot. Add tomato sauce, gravy and frozen potatoes. Bring to a boil; reduce heat to low. Cook 10 to 15 minutes until potatoes are tender.

Tiffany Nagem • Atlanta, Georgia

Cheese Steak and Tater Casserole

1½ pounds round steak
2 tablespoons flour
Salt and pepper
3 tablespoons butter
4 to 5 medium baking potatoes, peeled and diced
1 medium Vidalia onion, chopped
1 can tomato sauce
1 can cheese soup

Cube beef and dredge in flour seasoned with salt and pepper to taste. Heat butter in skillet and brown beef pieces on both sides. Add potatoes, onion, parsley, and salt and pepper to taste. Cook until edges of potatoes are browned. (Use some oil, if needed.) Transfer to casserole dish; pour tomato sauce and cheese soup over the top. Stir gently to coat all pieces. Cover and bake at 350° for about 1 hour. Serve hot.

Mandarin Beef on the Fly

½ pound thin-cut steaks, cut into strips
2 tablespoons soy sauce
1 teaspoon minced garlic
½ teaspoon sugar
¼ teaspoon crushed red pepper
⅛ teaspoon ground ginger
2 tablespoons vegetable oil
1 small can sliced water chestnuts
1 medium green bell pepper, sliced
1 small red bell pepper, sliced
1 carrot, sliced thin
2 cups cooked rice

Combine all ingredients in a skillet and cook over medium high heat until meat is cooked. Stir often and add more seasoning, if desired. Serve over cooked rice.

Sidney Lanier Bridge
Brunswick

Zesty Vidalia Onion Cube Steaks

½ cup self-rising flour
Salt and pepper
4 (4-ounce) cube steaks
2 teaspoons cooking oil
1 can diced tomatoes
1 cup tomato sauce
2 teaspoons oregano
2 teaspoons chili powder
½ teaspoon salt
½ teaspoon pepper
2 small green bell peppers, thinly sliced
1 medium Vidalia onion, sliced
1 box seasoned rice (like Uncle Bens),
   prepared per directions

Place flour in a shallow dish; add salt and pepper to taste. Dredge steaks in flour to coat both sides. In a large skillet, cook steaks in hot oil until browned. Stir in remaining ingredients, except rice. (Do not drain tomatoes.) Simmer, covered, for 25 minutes. Serve over prepared rice.

Vidalia Onion Festival
Vidalia • April

For more than 30 years, the Vidalia Onion Festival has celebrated the first harvest of the season of the world-famous Vidalia onion. The festival includes an airshow (featuring the U.S. Navy Blue Angels!), arts and crafts show, opening ceremonies (featuring the Swingin' Medallions and an amazing fireworks display), sweet onion cook-off, sweet-onion dish-tasting, Vidalia Onion Run 5K and 10K race, rodeo, carnival, and more.

912.538.8687
www.vidaliaonionfestival.com

Easy Beef Stew Casserole

2 cans beef stew
1 can mixed vegetables
1 tablespoon steak sauce
1 teaspoon black pepper
1 can refrigerator biscuits

Place beef stew, vegetables, steak sauce and pepper in a casserole dish; stir to mix well. Bake at 400° for about 20 minutes; remove from heat. Reduce heat to 350°. Place biscuits on top of stew and return to oven. Bake until biscuits are done.

Beef Stroganoff

Sauce

1 cup evaporated skim milk
1 tablespoon cornstarch
1 package onion-mushroom soup mix

Beef

1½ pounds beef, cubed
½ Vidalia onion, diced
1 garlic clove, minced
1½ cups fresh mushrooms, sliced
1 (8-ounce) container plain yogurt
3 to 4 cups hot cooked egg noodles

Combine evaporated milk and cornstarch in a large saucepan until smooth; stir in soup mix. Bring to a full boil, cover and reduce heat to low; simmer until beef mixture is ready. In a skillet, cook beef, onions and garlic until meat is browned. Stir in mushrooms; cook until onions and mushrooms should be tender. Add beef to sauce; stir well. Add yogurt and mix well; continue to simmer until everything is heated through. Server over noodles or mix them in.

Crockpot Sunday Roast

1 (3- to 5-pound) pot roast
2 cans cream of mushroom soup
1 package dry onion soup mix
1¼ cups water
5 carrots, sliced (1-inch pieces)
3 to 4 potatoes, peeled and cubed
1 small onion, quartered

Combine all ingredients in a large crockpot; cook on low 8 hours or high 4 hours.

Mega Roast Beef Swiss Dip Sandwich

1 loaf French bread, sliced in half horizontally
Butter, softened
1⅓ cups water
2 beef bullion cubes
1½ pounds thinly sliced deli roast beef
½ pound thinly sliced Swiss cheese
1 envelope onion soup mix

Spread butter evenly on French bread. In a saucepan, bring water to a boil and drop in bullion cubes. Turn off heat and let cubes dissolve; soak roast beef in batches. Drain excess moisture from meat then layer on bread. Continue until all meat is seasoned. Top meat with Swiss cheese and second half of bread. Bake at 350° until cheese is melted. While cooking, combine broth with onion soup mix; bring to a boil. As soon as it boils, reduce heat to simmer. Remove sandwich from oven when heated, slice into equal portions and serve with a side of sauce.

Poultry

Strawberry Glazed Chicken Drummettes with Strawberry Salsa

Strawberry Glazed Chicken Drummettes

20 small chicken drummettes
Salt, pepper, onion powder
1 (10-ounce) jar strawberry all-fruit
3 tablespoons Dijon mustard
1 tablespoon vegetable oil
2 teaspoons paprika
1 teaspoon ground mustard
1 teaspoon curry
3 tablespoons minced garlic

Jean Jackson won third place in the Georgia Strawberry Festival Strawberry Cook-Off with this great recipe!

Rinse chicken and pat dry. Season to taste with salt, pepper and onion powder; set aside. In a large bowl, combine strawberry all-fruit, Dijon mustard, vegetable oil, paprika, ground mustard, curry and minced garlic. Add drummettes and marinate in refrigerator 24 hours or overnight. Cook in oven preheated to 375°; brush with glaze several times during cooking. Cook 1 hour or until well browned and juices run clear when pierced with a fork. Serve hot or cold with Strawberry Salsa on the side.

Strawberry Salsa

1 cup thinly sliced red onion (about 1-inch long pieces)
3 medium vine-ripe tomatoes, chopped (about ¼- to ½-inch pieces)
3 cups chopped strawberries (about ¼- to ½-inch pieces)
3 tablespoons chopped cilantro
Salt and pepper

In a medium bowl, combine onion, tomatoes, strawberries and cilantro. Mix well; season to taste with salt and pepper. Chill until ready to serve.

Recipe by Jean Jackson
Submitted by Georgia Strawberry Festival

Crockpot BBQ Chicken Wings

5 pounds chicken wings with tips cut off
1 (12-ounce) bottle chili sauce
⅓ cup lemon juice
1 tablespoon Worcestershire sauce
2 tablespoons molasses
2 teaspoons salt
¼ teaspoon hot pepper sauce
1 dash garlic salt

Place wings in crockpot. Combine remaining ingredients and pour over chicken. Cook on low 6 to 8 hours or high 2 to 3 hours.

Peachy Chicken Wings

2 pounds chicken wings and drummies
1 can peaches
¼ cup hot sauce
1 stick (½ cup) melted butter
½ cup minced onion
½ tablespoon brown sugar

Break peaches into bits (use a chopper or blender, if desired). Combine peaches with remaining ingredients; add chicken and stir to cover all pieces. Marinate overnight, if possible. Remove chicken from marinade (discard marinade) and grill over medium heat or bake at 350° until done. Serve hot with ranch dressing or your favorite dipping sauces.

Georgia Peach Wings

Approximately 24 chicken wings
2 large Georgia peaches
½ teaspoon salt
¼ teaspoon pepper
2 teaspoons oil
1 tablespoon melted butter
2 teaspoons hot sauce
2 teaspoons honey
1 tablespoon red wine vinegar
2 tablespoons sliced green scallion
Garlic powder to taste

Rinse chicken wings and set aside. Peel peaches; mash. Combine with remaining ingredients. Add chicken and toss to coat evenly. Cover and chill overnight, if possible. Coat a large baking sheet with foil and spray with nonstick spray. Place wings on baking sheet leaving as much as sauce on the chicken as possible. Bake at 350° for about 20 minutes turning once to brown evenly. When chicken is done, remove from oven and serve hot.

Georgia Pecan-Crusted Chicken

1½ pounds chicken tenders
   (or boneless skinless chicken breasts)
1½ cups all-purpose flour
1 cup minced pecan halves
1 teaspoon salt
½ teaspoon pepper
2 large eggs
½ cup buttermilk
Lemon juice

*I am a pecan nut! (Pun intended.)
This quick recipe is great with Georgia
pecans or even sliced almonds.*

Wash chicken; set aside. Combine flour, pecans, salt and pepper; mix well. In a separate bowl, combine eggs, buttermilk and a dash of lemon juice. Dredge chicken in flour mixture, then in egg mixture, and then in flour mixture again. Place on a cooking sheet sprayed with nonstick spray. Give each piece of chicken a quick spray as well. Bake at 375° about 20 to 25 minutes depending on thickness of chicken. Serve hot.

Beer-Batter Fried Chicken

1 pound chicken tenders or boneless breasts
Salt and pepper
1 egg, beaten
1 beer
1 cup flour
⅓ cup minced Vidalia onion
Oil

Rinse chicken; season with salt and pepper. Combine egg, beer, flour and onion to make a batter similar to the consistency of pancake batter. Dredge chicken in the batter until coated well; fry in hot oil until golden brown and juices run clear. Serve hot.

Zesty Chicken Fajitas

1 pound boneless skinless chicken breasts or tenders
Oil
Minced garlic
Salt and pepper
½ cup Italian dressing
3 cups frozen stir-fry vegetables
2 teaspoons chili powder
Salsa
1 cup shredded Cheddar cheese
8 to 10 flour tortillas

In a nonstick skillet, cook chicken in a small amount of oil; sprinkle with dashes of garlic, salt and pepper. Break or shred chicken into large chunks as it cooks. When chicken is done, add Italian dressing, vegetables and chili powder. Simmer until vegetables are cooked. Serve hot with salsa and cheese on flour tortillas.

Fiesta Georgia
Suwanee • September

Atlanta's largest Hispanic Heritage Month outdoor celebration, Fiesta Georgia takes place in September at Stone Mountain Park. Over 15,000 people are expected to attend Atlanta's annual Hispanic Heritage Month celebration. Fiesta Georgia is a day long celebration of Latino culture, music, and food. It will feature continuous live performances by national and local artists, vendor booths offering free product samples, arts and crafts, and authentic Latino foods.

770.945.8996 • www.suwanee.com

Baked Cheesy Chicken and Broccoli

2 pounds boneless chicken, cubed
Olive oil
1 package frozen broccoli
1 (6-ounce) package cornmeal stuffing mix
1 can cream of mushroom soup
1 can Cheddar cheese soup
½ cup shredded white American cheese
½ cup Parmesan cheese
½ cup chopped onion
Salt and pepper

Brown edges, but don't fully cook, chicken in a skillet with a small amount of olive oil. Thaw and drain broccoli. Combine all ingredients in a large baking dish; bake at 400° 30 to 35 minutes or until top starts to bubble and brown. Serve hot.

Jeff Kinsey • shutterstock.com

Chicken Teriyaki & Rice

¼ cup Italian dressing
1 pound boneless skinless chicken, cubed
⅔ cup chopped Vidalia onion
⅓ cup water
¼ teaspoon pepper
⅓ cup soy sauce
¼ cup brown sugar
½ teaspoon garlic powder
½ teaspoon ground ginger
⅓ cup balsamic vinegar
2 cups frozen broccoli
1½ cups instant rice, uncooked

Heat Italian dressing in a large nonstick skillet over medium-high heat. Add chicken, onion, water, pepper, soy sauce, brown sugar, garlic powder, ginger and vinegar. Cook, stirring frequently, about 10 minutes. When chicken is done, add broccoli and rice. Cook until rice is done adding more water, if needed. Serve hot.

Sautéed Creamy Chicken

6 chicken breasts
Oil
1 tablespoon minced onion
1 bottle Italian dressing
¼ cup milk
1 cup sour cream

In a skillet cook chicken in a small amount of oil and onion to brown edges. Stir in Italian dressing and milk; continue to cook until chicken is done, adding water if necessary. Remove chicken to a platter. Stir sour cream into juices in skillet to make a sauce adding additional water to desired consistency. Pour sauce over chicken; serve hot.

Savannah Chicken with Garlic Sauce

4 to 6 chicken breasts
Olive oil
2 large tomatoes, diced
½ cup chopped red onion
2 tablespoons lemon juice
2 garlic cloves, finely chopped
3 tablespoons chopped fresh basil
¼ teaspoon crushed hot red pepper flakes
¼ teaspoon salt
⅛ teaspoon ground black pepper

Garlic Sauce

1 cup sour cream
1 tablespoon mayonnaise
½ tablespoon minced garlic
1 tablespoon water or milk
Parsley flakes
Dash oregano

Brush chicken with olive oil, place in a glass baking dish, and set aside. In a medium bowl, combine tomatoes, onion, lemon juice, garlic, basil, red pepper, salt and pepper; pour over chicken. Lightly cover with foil and bake at 350° 30 to 45 minutes or until juices run clear. Combine sauce ingredients; add more water or milk for desired thickness. Serve chicken hot with sauce drizzled over top.

Augusta Oven-Fried Pecan Chicken

Chicken

6 boneless chicken breasts
½ cup buttermilk
⅓ cup mustard
1 egg
⅓ cup cornmeal
¼ cup flour
1½ cups finely chopped Georgia pecans
½ teaspoon salt
½ teaspoon pepper

While traveling back from the Masters Golf Tournament in Augusta, Georgia, several years ago, I stopped at a small restaurant. The restaurant is now long gone but this great dish they served lives on.

Sauce

⅔ cup creamy ranch dressing
1 tablespoon mustard
1 tablespoon mayonnaise
1 tablespoon milk
Dash Worcestershire sauce

Rinse chicken breasts and pat dry; cut into serving-size pieces. Combine buttermilk, mustard and egg; beat to mix well. Combine remaining chicken ingredients in a separate bowl. Dip chicken in dry mixture, then in egg mixture, and then in dry mixture again to coat well. Bake on a baking sheet coated with nonstick spray in a 375° oven about 30 minutes. Combine sauce ingredients in a small bowl. Serve chicken hot with sauce on the side or drizzled over the top.

Vidalia Onion Chicken

4 to 6 chicken breasts
1 Vidalia onion, sliced
⅔ cup soy sauce
½ cup bourbon
1 teaspoon garlic powder
1 teaspoon ground ginger
4 tablespoons olive oil
¼ cup brown sugar

Combine all ingredients in a bowl and toss to coat evenly. Transfer chicken and sauce a nonstick skillet. Add a small amount of olive oil and brown chicken over medium heat. Onions should soften as well. Cook until juices run clear. Serve chicken covered in Vidalia onions.

Riverwalk
Augusta

Augusta Convention & Visitors Bureau

Vidalia Stuffed Chicken Breasts

4 to 6 chicken breasts, butterflied
Olive oil
Salt, pepper and Italian seasoning

Stuffing

1 cup chopped Vidalia onion
1 yellow bell pepper, chopped
1 red bell pepper, chopped
1 tablespoon apple butter or sauce
3 tablespoons lime juice
2 tablespoons chicken broth
½ teaspoon cumin
⅛ teaspoon red pepper
1 teaspoon minced garlic

Rub chicken with olive oil. Sprinkle with salt, pepper and Italian seasoning to taste. In a separate bowl, combine stuffing ingredients and mix well. Arrange chicken pieces evenly in a casserole dish coated with nonstick spray (without the sides touching other pieces of chicken, if possible). Spoon equal portions stuffing into each breast and secure with a toothpick, if needed. Add a few tablespoons water to the dish and cover with foil. Bake about 20 minutes at 350°. Uncover, brush with a small amount of butter and continue to cook 5 to 10 minutes or until done and golden brown. Serve hot.

Barbara's Sweet Onion & Peppers Chicken Pasta

1 medium Vidalia onion, sliced into rings
1 medium red bell pepper, cut into thin strips
1 medium yellow bell pepper, cut into thin strips
1 teaspoon minced garlic
4 to 6 tablespoons butter
2 chicken breasts, cubed
2 tablespoons tarragon
¾ cup half & half or heavy cream
1 cup shredded mozzarella cheese
½ cup Parmesan cheese
8 ounces angel hair pasta, cooked

Cook onions, peppers and garlic in butter until soft. Remove onions and peppers; set aside. Add chicken and tarragon to pan; cook until chicken is brown. Add cream, reserved onions and peppers and cheeses. Simmer until cheese is melted. Add pasta.

Barbara Hall
Rocky Face, Georgia

Chicken 'n Bacon Pasta

1½ cups uncooked pasta noodles
½ cup mayonnaise
½ cup chopped Vidalia onion
⅓ cup milk
½ teaspoon salt
½ teaspoon dried basil
2 cups frozen mixed vegetables, thawed
1½ cups cubed cooked chicken
1 cup cooked and crumbled bacon
1½ cups shredded Cheddar cheese, divided

Cook noodles per directions on package. Combine with remaining ingredients in an oven-safe dish; bake at 325° until top is golden brown.

Georgia Blueberry Chicken Spread

2 cups fresh Georgia blueberries
2 cups cubed cooked chicken breast
½ cup chopped celery
½ cup chopped red bell pepper
⅓ cup sliced green onions
¼ cup chopped Georgia pecans
1 single-serving cup lemon yogurt
3 tablespoons mayonnaise
½ teaspoon salt

Combine all ingredients in a large bowl. Cover and chill before serving.

Nacho Chicken Stuffed Bell Pepper

6 green bell peppers
1½ pounds cooked shredded chicken
1 cup cooked rice
1 small can green chilies
1 can chili
½ cup crumbled tortilla chips
½ cup chopped onion
½ cup shredded cheese
Salt and pepper
½ tablespoon garlic powder

Slice peppers in half, remove core, and set aside. Combine remaining ingredients. Mix well; spoon into bell pepper halves. Arrange stuffed peppers in a baking pan or casserole dish coated with nonstick spray. Bake at 350° 20 to 25 minutes. Top with additional cheese, if desired. Serve hot.

Chicken Quarters and Goober Sauce

4 chicken quarters with skin
Soy sauce
Pepper
Ginger

Goober Sauce

1 cup peanuts
1½ tablespoons oil
1 teaspoon garlic powder
1 teaspoon sugar
2 tablespoons soy sauce
½ tablespoon lime juice
1 to 2 tablespoons hot pepper flakes, optional

Brush chicken with soy sauce; sprinkle with pepper and ginger. Bake at 350° until juices run clear and skin has crisped. While chicken is cooking, combine peanuts and oil in a food processor. Mix until the consistency of peanut butter. Add remaining ingredients. Stir in water to desired consistency, if needed. Add hot pepper flakes for added kick, if desired. Serve chicken hot with Goober Sauce on the side.

Plains Peanut Festival
Plains • Fourth weekend in September

The annual Plains Peanut Festival is centered around one of the Sumter County community's claims to fame—its peanut production. The festival features the community's most famous residents, President and Mrs. Carter, in active roles throughout the weekend. Fun events include a one-mile fun run, a 5K road race, and a parade. Food and craft vendors sell their unique merchandise, while local entertainment acts perform throughout the afternoon. Visitors may also view educational exhibits that accent the importance of agriculture in this region.

229.824.5373 • www.plainsgeorgia.com

Photo courtesy jerrybattle.com

Georgia

BBQ Chicken Thighs

1 bottle barbecue sauce
1 bottle beer
1 stick (½ cup) butter
1 cup water
1 Vidalia onion, finely chopped
10 to 12 chicken thighs

In a large pot, combine barbecue sauce, beer, butter and water; add chicken. Simmer about 25 minutes. Remove chicken (discard sauce) and grill about 10 minutes over high heat to brown edges. (Do not overcook or chicken will dry out.) Serve hot. You can also bake this chicken uncovered in a 350° oven until done.

President Jimmy Carter signs his book at Plains Peanut Festival.

Photo courtesy jerrybattle.com

My Aunt's Favorite Roasted Chicken

3 to 4 lemons
8 large garlic cloves, minced
2 teaspoons dried thyme
1 tablespoon paprika
1½ teaspoons ground cumin
¾ teaspoon cayenne pepper
2 (3-pound) chickens, split lengthwise
Salt and pepper

Slice lemons in half. Squeeze enough lemons to get ¾ cup lemon juice; slice remaining lemons in half again and set aside. Whisk lemon juice, minced garlic, thyme, paprika, cumin and cayenne pepper in small bowl. Place chicken in 9x13-inch glass baking dish. Pour marinade over chicken coating completely. Cover and refrigerate at least 6 hours or overnight. Preheat oven to 425°. Transfer chicken and marinade to large roasting pan; season with salt and pepper. Bake, basting occasionally, about 50 minutes or until chicken is golden brown and cooked through. Transfer chicken to plates. Garnish with reserved lemon wedges. Serve with rice using the pan juices as a gravy or sauce for the rice.

Seth Bush

Seth says, "My Aunt lived just north of Atlanta in Conyers, Georgia; this is her favorite roasted chicken dish."

Southern Fried Chicken

1 chicken, cut up
1 cup all-purpose flour
2 teaspoons seasoning salt
1 teaspoon freshly ground pepper
1 teaspoon garlic powder
½ teaspoon sugar
Vegetable oil

Nothing beats some good fried chicken from Georgia. The secret is hot oil. When using a skillet, make sure the sides are deep enough to avoid splashing.

Wash and lightly dry chicken pieces. Combine remaining ingredients in a zip-close bag and mix well. Add chicken 1 or 2 pieces at a time; shake to coat. Drop in hot oil and fry until golden brown. Drain on paper towels for 2 minutes before serving.

Country-Style Shake and Bake Chicken

2 to 3 pounds chicken (assorted pieces)

Marinade

2 teaspoons hot sauce
2 teaspoons honey
2 teaspoons soy sauce
4 tablespoons melted butter

Coating

3 cups flour
1 cup cornmeal
3 cups crushed saltine crackers
3 tablespoons salt
2 tablespoons sugar
2 teaspoons garlic powder
2 teaspoons onion powder
3 tablespoons paprika

Rinse chicken; set aside. Combine marinade ingredients in a small bowl. Combine coating ingredients in a zip-close or paper bag. Brush each piece of chicken with a light coating of marinade. Place 2 to 3 pieces of chicken into bag with flour mixture. Close top tightly and shake until well coated; place on nonstick baking sheet. Repeat until all chicken is coated. Use remaining coating mixture to coat bare spots on any pieces. Bake in a 400° oven until juices run clear. Serve hot and crispy.

Spice-Rubbed Baked Game Hens

4 small game hens
Olive oil
1 tablespoon salt
1 tablespoon black pepper
1 teaspoon celery salt
4 teaspoons paprika
1 tablespoon garlic powder
1 tablespoon Italian seasoning
4 teaspoons dried thyme
1 teaspoon ground ginger
½ teaspoon dried basil

Clean hens and rub with olive oil. Combine remaining ingredients into a rub. Rub each bird with rub mixture and place in a cooking dish. Spray very lightly with nonstick spray; gently cover with foil. Bake at 350° about 35 minutes or until juices run clear (cooking time will vary depending on the size of the bird). Remove foil the last few minutes of cooking to brown. Serve hot.

This recipe is perfect for hens bought at the store or for your favorite wild game. Georgia has plenty of wild game birds and this recipe would work with any of them.

Southeastern Cowboy Gathering

Cartersville • Second weekend of March

The Booth Western Art Museum, located in Cartersville, Georgia, hosts the Annual Southeastern Cowboy Gathering the second weekend of every March. The four day celebration of the West includes a special presentation by a featured artist; the End of Trail Concert; the annual Southeastern Chuck Wagon Cook-Off; an old time mandolin, banjo, flat picking guitar, and fiddle contest; a special concert by a featured entertainer; cowboy poetry and music; a Dutch Oven Cook-Off; Cowboy Church; and a host of family entertainment and children's activities.

770.387.1300 • www.boothmuseum.org

Southern Fried Turkey

1 whole turkey, thawed
1 bottle beer
½ bottle hot sauce
1 or 2 taco or chili seasoning packets

Fill a large fryer with water. Drop turkey into water (excess water will spill over); remaining amount of water will give you a good idea how much oil you need. Remove turkey and pat dry. Heat oil in fryer to 350° per directions. (Never cook on a wooden deck, under a carport or in a garage. I suggest placing a protective cover over concrete to protect from stains.) Make sure your turkey is as dry as possible on the outside. Combine beer, hot sauce and seasoning. (You can add an additional seasoning pack to the oil, if desired.) Mix until dissolved and inject into turkey using an injector. Fry at 350° about 3 to 4 minutes per pound. Remove from heat and allow to rest about 20 minutes before carving.

Tasting the Beans at the Southeastern Cowboy Gathering in Cartersville

Baked Pecan Whole Turkey

1 turkey, thawed with neck and packets removed
2 teaspoons salt
2 teaspoons pepper
2 teaspoons Cajun seasoning
2 stalks celery, chopped
1 medium Vidalia onion
Rosemary and thyme to taste
⅔ cup chopped Georgia pecans
Butter

Rinse turkey with cool water. Place in baking pan and rub skin evenly with butter. Sprinkle with the salt, pepper, Cajun seasoning, celery, onion, rosemary, thyme and pecans. Cover and bake at 450° about 20 minutes. Reduce heat to 325° and bake an additional 15 minutes per pound or until internal temp reads 170° in the breast and 180° in the thigh.

Baked Turkey Burgers

1½ pounds ground turkey
1 egg
1 cup breadcrumbs
½ cup minced onion
½ teaspoon minced garlic
½ cup packed fresh parsley leaves
¾ teaspoon salt
½ teaspoon black pepper
½ tablespoon soy sauce
1 tablespoon yellow mustard

Combine all ingredients and form into patties. Bake at 350° until juice runs clear. Serve hot on hamburger buns with your favorite toppings.

Fish & Seafood

Soppin' Shrimp

5 pounds shrimp, in shell and not cooked
6 lemons, thinly sliced (rind and all)
1 (1-pint) bottle Italian salad dressing
1 pound butter or Fleischman's lite margarine, melted
Coarse ground pepper to taste
6 garlic cloves (optional)

Preheat oven to 350°. Mix all ingredients together in large casserole or broiler pan. Cover and bake 30 to 40 minutes, stirring ½ way through for even cooking. Do not overcook! Serve the "cooking juice" in individual bowls with French bread to "SOP" in juice plus tossed salad, corn on cob or broccoli to make a meal.

Melba Sorrell Locher
Hahira, Georgia

Tossed Tangy Shrimp Cocktail Platter

2 pounds large Georgia shrimp,
  cooked and deveined
Creole seasoning
½ cup ketchup
⅓ cup lime juice
3 teaspoons hot sauce
1 tablespoon Worcestershire sauce

Tomato wedges
Sliced carrots
Sliced celery
Flavored crackers
½ cup chopped onion
2 avocados, chopped

Sprinkle cooked shrimp with Creole seasoning. Combine ketchup, lime juice, hot sauce and Worcestershire sauce in a small bowl. On a platter, arrange shrimp with veggies and crackers around bowl of sauce.

Wild Georgia Shrimp Cocktail Shrimp

4 pounds Wild Georgia Shrimp
1 lemon
2 tablespoons butter or olive oil
2 tablespoons coarse salt
2 tablespoons black pepper

Place shrimp in a pot just big enough to fit snugly. Squeeze lemon over shrimp and drop lemon halves in pot. Add remaining ingredients and cover with water by 1 inch. Bring to a boil over high heat. As soon as water boils, remove from heat. Allow to sit 3 minutes; drain. Allow shrimp to cool before serving with your favorite cocktail sauce.

Courtesy of Hunter Forsyth
Submitted by Wild Georgia Shrimp

Hunter Forsyth and his wife Suzanne are lifelong residents of Valona, Georgia. He says he prefers to leave the head on the shrimp for this simple recipe. The small piece of fat between the shrimp's body and head adds flavor.

Oven-Roasted Shrimp in Olive Oil

1 pound Wild Georgia Shrimp,
  peeled and deveined
¼ cup olive oil
1 teaspoon garlic powder
½ teaspoon salt
½ teaspoon freshly ground black pepper
Juice of 1 lemon

Place shrimp in a glass bowl. Add olive oil, garlic powder, salt and pepper; toss to coat. Cover with plastic wrap and refrigerate at least 1 hour. Remove shrimp from refrigerator, squeeze juice of lemon over top, and let stand 30 minutes before baking. Preheat oven to 400°. Bake about 2 minutes on each side, or until shrimp turn opaque.

Courtesy of Suzanne & Hunter Forsyth
Submitted by Wild Georgia Shrimp

This quick and easy recipe comes from Suzanne Forsyth dock master of Valona Seafood in Valona, Georgia, which she owns with her husband, Hunter. For easier clean up, she tosses all the ingredients in a plastic zip bag to marinate.

Jekyll Island Shrimp & Grits Festival

Jekyll Island • September

This weekend festival is for anyone who loves coastal cuisine and southern cooking. Shrimp & Grits is the highlighted dish in a festival that features a cooking competition, shrimp boat excursion, and shrimp eating contests. To round out the event, guests can visit our arts, crafts, and antique vendor area, listen to live music and visit the Kids Fun Zone. Admission to the festival is free.

912.635.4189
www.jekyllisland.com/shrimpandgrits

Broiled Jumbo Shrimp Parmesan

4 pounds Jumbo shrimp from Georgia coast
1 cup Italian salad dressing
Grated Parmesan cheese

Peel and devein shrimp. In a zip-close bag, combine shrimp with salad dressing. Coat evenly, close bag and chill 1 to 2 hours. Remove shrimp from marinade (discard marinade). Place shrimp on a nonstick cookie sheet and sprinkle evenly with Parmesan cheese. Broil in oven, turning once, until shrimp is no longer fleshy. Serve hot with noodles or rice.

Shrimp Peeling Competition
Shrimp & Grits Festival
Jekyll Island

Grilled Shrimp and Green Beans with Basil Vinaigrette

Basil Vinaigrette

½ cup balsamic vinegar
½ cup chopped fresh basil
4 large shallots, minced
3 garlic cloves, minced
1 tablespoon brown sugar
1 teaspoon seasoned pepper
½ teaspoon salt
1 cup olive oil

Whisk together all ingredients, except olive oil, until blended. Gradually add olive oil, whisking constantly until blended.

Grilled Shrimp and Green Beans

1½ pounds fresh green beans
2 pounds peeled medium-sized raw shrimp
Basil Vinaigrette, divided
6 bacon slices, cooked and crumbled
1½ cups shredded Parmesan cheese
¾ cup chopped almonds

Cook beans in boiling salted water 4 minutes or until crisp-tender. Drain then plunge into ice water to stop the cooking process; drain, pat dry and set aside. Combine shrimp and ¾ cup Basil Vinaigrette in a large zip-close plastic bag; chill 15 minutes. Remove shrimp; discard all but 2 tablespoons marinade. Cook shrimp in skillet over medium-high heat with 2 tablespoons marinade until pink. Toss shrimp with green beans, bacon, cheese, almonds, and remaining Vinaigrette. Serves 4 to 6.

Georgia

Georgia Coast
Spicy Shrimp Sandwich Spread

1½ pounds small Wild Georgia Shrimp
½ cup mayonnaise
⅓ cup chopped celery
⅓ cup chopped carrots
⅓ cup finely chopped onion
¼ cup chopped almonds
2 teaspoons Cajun seasoning
½ teaspoon black pepper
2 teaspoons lemon juice
¼ teaspoon Worcestershire sauce

Cook, peel and devein shrimp. In a large bowl, combine shrimp with remaining ingredients. Use more mayonnaise, if desired. If larger shrimp are used, you can cut them in half. Don't be worried if shrimp break apart slightly while mixing. Chill and serve on your favorite bread. Add lettuce and tomato, if desired.

Crawdad Finger Sandwiches

2 pounds packaged minced crawfish meat
½ tablespoon Italian seasoning
½ cup diced celery
½ cup sweet relish
¼ cup minced onion
½ cup mayonnaise
1 tablespoon lemon juice
Salt and pepper

Cook meat per package directions; cool. Combine with remaining ingredients and mix with a spoon. Chill and spread over bread or crackers.

Easy Georgia Crawdaddy Étouffée

1½ pounds frozen crawfish, thawed
1 can cream of mushroom soup
1 can cream of celery soup
1 cup water
½ Vidalia onion, finely chopped
2 green bell peppers, chopped
1 red bell pepper, chopped
1 tablespoon minced garlic

½ stick butter
2 tablespoons parsley flakes
2 tablespoons Cajun seasoning
Salt and Pepper
Hot sauce
Crushed red pepper flakes
3 to 4 cups cooked rice

In a large pot, combine meat, soups and water over medium heat. In a large skillet, sauté onions, bell peppers, and garlic in butter until veggies are tender; add to pot along with remaining ingredients. Reduce heat. Cover and cook until mixture thickens. Serve over hot rice.

Grilled Georgia Catfish and Tropical Fruit Salsa

Grilled Georgia Catfish

4 catfish fillets
2 tablespoons olive oil
1 teaspoon minced garlic
½ teaspoon kosher salt
½ teaspoon ground black pepper
¼ teaspoon crushed red pepper

Brush each fillet with oil. Combine garlic, salt pepper, and red pepper. Sprinkle over fillets. Grill fish until it flakes easily with a fork.

Tropical Fruit Salsa

1 cup diced mango
1 tablespoon chopped cilantro
1 tablespoon minced jalapeño
2 tablespoons fresh lime juice
1 tablespoon honey

Combine well. Serve over Grilled Georgia Catfish.

Scott Herpst
Walker County Messenger

Kingsland Fried Catfish

3 to 4 medium pieces catfish per person
1 cup yellow cornmeal (or enough to coat fillets)
2 teaspoons Lawry's seasoned salt
   per 1 cup cornmeal
Vegetable cooking oil (enough to cover fish)

The secret to fried catfish is cooking at just the right temperature to seal in moisture and flavor. Rinse fillets thoroughly in cool water; pat dry with paper towel. Mix cornmeal and seasoned salt; coat fillets with mixture. Lay on paper towels to set coating. Place enough oil in deep-fryer or large pan to cover fillets. Heat oil to 325°. Gently place fillets in oil and fry until golden brown, about 5 minutes. Remove from oil and place a paper towel to absorb excess oil. Serve with coleslaw, hush puppies and sweet tea ("the Champagne of the South").

Kingsland Labor Day Catfish Festival

Kingsland Labor Day Catfish Festival

Nothing goes better with crispy southern-fried catfish than a succulent serving of country music. And festival goers can feast on this and much more during Kingsland, Georgia's Annual Labor Day Weekend Catfish Festival in historic downtown. Scheduled events include a parade, arts and crafts booths, Southern fried and Cajun catfish, a variety of food booths, antiques and collectibles, and children's amusement area.

800.433.0225 • www.VisitKingsland.com

Country Fried Spicy Catfish

2 cups white cornmeal
½ cup flour
Salt, pepper, and garlic powder
1 tablespoon hot sauce
6 to 8 catfish fillets
Oil for frying

Spicy Dipping Sauce

¾ cup sour cream
¼ cup mayo
½ teaspoon salt
½ teaspoon ground black pepper
1 onion, finely chopped
Large dash garlic powder
1 tablespoon parsley
Hot sauce, if desired

Combine cornmeal, flour, salt and pepper to taste and a dash of garlic powder in a shallow plate. Dredge catfish in hot sauce and then in cornmeal mix. Fry in hot oil until golden brown. Mix dipping sauce in a small bowl and serve on the side.

Labor Day Catfish Festival Parade
Kingsland

Georgia Hot Fish 'n Tots

20 pieces fish fillets
Hot sauce
2 cups cornmeal
1 cup flour
2 teaspoons salt
1 teaspoon black pepper
A few clean paper grocery bags
Frozen tater tots
Cajun seasoning

In a large bowl, gently coat fish with hot sauce. Combine cornmeal, flour, salt and pepper in grocery bag or large zip-close bag. Shake to mix thoroughly. Drop fish in bag, fold top and shake to bread fish. Deep fry fish in hot oil until golden brown. Fry tater tots in same oil and sprinkle with Cajun seasoning while still hot. Serve hot with tartar sauce for dipping and a side of coleslaw.

St. Simon Fried Grouper Sandwich

4 grouper fillets, cleaned
1 tablespoon lemon juice
1 teaspoon hot sauce
1 teaspoon soy sauce
½ cup flour

1 teaspoon salt
1 teaspoon pepper
Butter
Buns
Sandwich Fixin's

Brush fish with lemon juice, hot sauce and soy sauce. Combine flour, salt and pepper in a shallow dish; dredge fish to coat lightly. Fry grouper in about ¼-inch melted butter until fish flakes with fork. Serve on your favorite style bun with your favorite fixings.

Scott Hunsucker

North Georgia Pan-Seared Trout

4 trout fillets
Lemon juice
½ cup cornmeal
1 teaspoon salt
1 teaspoon pepper
2 teaspoons Italian seasoning
Oil

Rinse trout in cool water; DO NOT pat dry. Sprinkle a small amount of lemon juice over each fillet. Combine cornmeal, salt, pepper and Italian seasoning. Dredge moist trout into breading to lightly coat each fillet. Heat oil in a skillet and pan-fry trout only long enough to brown each side evenly to a light golden color. Remove trout from frying pan and place in shallow baking pan lined with foil; bake in a 350° oven about 20 minutes. Serve hot with your favorite sides.

Scott's Grilled Georgia Coast Shark Steak

4 fresh shark steaks, 1 inch thick
⅔ cup soy sauce
2 freshly squeezed limes
1 freshly squeezed lemon
Dash (or three) salt
Freshly ground pepper
Dash lemon pepper
Spanish rosemary, optional
Olive oil

Mix soy sauce, lime and lemon juice, salt, pepper, lemon pepper and rosemary in a plastic zip-close bag big enough to hold steaks. Lightly coat steaks with olive oil; add to marinade. Refrigerate 2 to 3 hours. Heat grill to high then reduce to medium-high. Brush some olive oil on a fish basket and put steaks in it. Cook shark about 4 minutes on each side or until it flakes.

Scott Hunsucker

Sweet Vidalia Onion and Seafood Pasta

8 ounces fettuccine, uncooked
½ cup soy sauce
¼ cup rice wine vinegar
¼ cup water
1 teaspoon ground ginger
1 tablespoon oriental sesame oil
½ teaspoon crushed red pepper
Salt and pepper
1½ large Vidalia onions, sliced
1 red bell pepper, diced
2 teaspoons cornstarch
1 pound shrimp, crab or favorite seafood
Butter or oil
2 tablespoons parsley
½ cup crushed croutons

Cook fettuccine according to package directions; drain and set aside. Combine soy sauce, vinegar, water, ginger, sesame oil, red pepper, and salt and pepper to taste. Stir in onions and bell pepper to coat evenly; cook in a skillet with cornstarch until onions begin to soften. Stir in seafood and continue to cook. Add a bit of butter or olive oil, as needed. Combine fettuccine, parsley, and seafood mixture; toss gently to coat everything with crouton crumbs. Serve hot.

Savannah Seafood Festival

Savannah • October

Everyone loves fresh seafood and that's exactly what the Savannah Seafood Festival is all about. Sample fresh wild Georgia Shrimp, blue crabs or grouper while you browse among unique arts and crafts. You might even be tempted to take part in the annual "Mullet Toss" contest...yes, with real mullets! Come and take home some delicious Savannah memories.

912.234.0295
www.riverstreetsavannah.com

Pan-Seared Scallops

2 pounds bay scallops
Olive oil
½ cup chopped Georgia pecans
⅓ cup parsley
½ tablespoon minced garlic
1 teaspoon lemon juice
½ tablespoon soy sauce
½ cup all-purpose flour
½ cup cornmeal
2 tablespoons olive oil
1 tablespoon orange juice

Gently brush scallops with olive oil; set aside. Combine pecans, parsley, garlic, lemon juice and soy sauce; set aside. Sprinkle flour and cornmeal over scallops and toss to evenly coat; discard excess coating. Heat 2 tablespoons olive oil in a large skillet over medium heat; add scallops. When scallops are hot, but not yet browning, add pecan mixture; cook until scallops are golden brown. Serve hot.

Mullet Toss
Savannah Seafood Festival

Oven-Broiled Oysters

¼ cup butter or margarine
3 tablespoons flour
1 garlic clove, minced
1 tablespoon onion juice (or minced onion)
1 tablespoon Worcestershire sauce
¼ teaspoon celery seed
¾ cup liquid (from oysters or water)
1 (2-ounce) can mushrooms
18 medium shrimp
1½ pints medium oysters, reserve shells
Parmesan cheese
Rock Salt

To make sauce, melt butter and add flour, garlic, onion juice, Worcestershire sauce, celery seed and liquid. Add mushrooms and shrimp. Cook until thickened and shrimp are pink. In a separate saucepan, simmer oysters just until edges curl; drain. Put on cleaned oyster shells. Cover each with sauce mixture then sprinkle with cheese. Place on tray covered with rock salt. Broil in a hot oven about 5 minutes or until bubbly.

Stuffed Baked Lobster

1 or 2 (or more) lobsters
4 tablespoons butter
1 garlic clove, chopped
1 egg
1 cup stuffing mix
¼ teaspoon oregano
Pinch sweet basil (or lemon pepper,
  or Italian seasoning, or whatever you like)
Salt and pepper to taste
Half & half

Measurements are for 1 or 2 lobster; double for 3 to 4 lobster. Remove lobster from freezer and defrost in refrigerator (will take several hours). After lobster is thawed, place on back and cut belly through to end of tail. Do not cut completely through. With a fork, remove stuff close to the head and throw out. Spoon out the row and the rest of the stuff in the belly (if there is black stuff, throw it out; it doesn't add anything to the meal and it looks ugly); set aside. Melt butter in a skillet over medium heat; sauté garlic until it starts to brown, do not burn. Add egg; stir. Add stuffing, oregano, sweet basil, and salt and pepper to taste; mix well. Combine with reserved lobster meat; add enough half & half to make mixture moist. Place lobsters on their backs and spoon stuffing into stomach cavity until filled and bulging above the shell. (If you have left-over stuffing, freeze for the next time.) Place in a preheated oven at 350° and bake 30 minutes.

Chuck Lanham
St. Marys, Georgia

Freezing Lobster for Future Use

Wait for a sale on lobsters; you'll never have to pay full price if you plan ahead. Trust me, this works. Using this technique, you'll make lobster that tastes just like those you get in a restaurant. When you find a sale, purchase as many lobsters as you think you will use in the next couple months—1½ pounds is a usual one-serving portion (unless you are a big eater). Regardless of size, all lobsters have the same tenderness and texture.

If you have time to wait, have the market steam the lobsters. If not, bring them home and prepare them right away. Place enough water in a pot to almost cover lobsters. (You may need to do this in batches, depending on the number of lobsters you buy). Bring water to a boil and place lobsters in water. Bring back to boil, reduce heat to continue a slow boil. Continue cooking 8 to 10 minutes, depending on size of lobster. Remove from boiling water and place under running cold water. After lobsters are cooled, place in a plastic bag, seal, and place in the freezer unless you are eating that night, then just wrap in plastic and put in the fridge. If the store steamed them for you, just seal and place in freezer, after cooled.

Deep Fried Georgia Crab Puppies

5 slices white bread
1½ pounds minced crab
4 bacon strips, cooked and crumbled
½ medium onion, minced
1 teaspoon salt
2 teaspoons black pepper
½ cup cornmeal
3 eggs, beaten
¼ cup milk
4 tablespoons cornstarch
Oil for frying

A cross between a crab cake and a hushpuppy... yum!

Break bread into tiny pieces; mix with remaining ingredients, except oil. Use additional milk, if needed. (Mixture should be firm enough to hold a hushpuppy shape.) Using a spoon, form dough into balls; fry in hot oil until golden brown. Serve hot.

Beach Walk on
St. Simon Island

J. L. White • RandomFox.com

Cornbread Crab Cakes

Crab Cakes

½ cup mayonnaise
2 eggs, beaten
¼ cup diced scallions
2 teaspoons Worcestershire sauce
1 teaspoon mustard
¼ teaspoon black pepper
1 tablespoon parsley
2½ cups cornbread stuffing mix
12 ounces frozen or imitation crabmeat
1 small can corn, drained
Chunky salsa
Vegetable oil

White Sauce

3 tablespoons sour cream
2 tablespoons mayonnaise
1 tablespoon milk
1 tablespoon Italian seasoning

Combine crab cake ingredients, except oil and salsa. Form into 8 to 10 equal-sized patties and place on wax paper. Chill about 30 minutes to set. Combine white sauce ingredients in a small bowl; chill. Thin with additional milk, if needed, so sauce is thin enough to drizzle over crab cakes. In a colander, drain salsa leaving all of the chunky vegetables. Heat oil in a large skillet over medium heat. Sauté crab cake patties until golden brown on each side. Drain on paper towels. Serve hot topped with drained salsa and drizzled with white sauce.

Georgia Pecan Seafood Cakes

2 cans salmon, cleaned and drained
1 pound white fish, cooked and flaked
8 to 10 Ritz crackers, crumbled
1 tablespoon real bacon bits
1 egg, beaten
3 tablespoons olive oil
2 tablespoons butter
¼ cup minced onion
¼ cup minced bell pepper
¼ cup unbleached flour
1 cup half and half
1½ tablespoons Dijon mustard
2 teaspoons hot chili sauce
2 tablespoons lemon juice
1 cup toasted Georgia pecans
3 slices whole wheat bread, crumbled
1 teaspoon fresh cracked black pepper

When visiting the Georgia coast, I enjoyed some delicious seafood cakes coated in a pecan mix. This recipe is best served with tartar sauce mixed with a bit of horseradish.

Combine all ingredients, except pecans, bread and pepper. Chill; form into equal-sized cakes. In a food processor, combine pecans, bread and pepper. Sprinkle over each cake press gently in with fingers. On a prepared or nonstick cookie sheet, bake at 400° about 10 to 11 minutes. Serve hot.

Cookies & Candies

Rose Anne's Toffee Pecan Cookies

2 cups all-purpose flour
1 teaspoon salt
½ teaspoon baking powder
½ teaspoon baking soda
1 cup rolled oats
½ cup chopped pecans
1 stick (½ cup) butter
1 cup honey
½ cup sour cream
2 teaspoons vanilla extract
8 ounces chopped dates or raisins
½ cup toffee chips

This recipe won a blue ribbon at the 2006 Eastern Apiculture Society Honey Show for the cookie division.

Combine flour, salt, baking powder, baking soda, oats and pecans in a small bowl; set aside. In a large bowl, cream butter and mix in honey until well blended. Stir in sour cream and vanilla. Blend in flour mixture and remaining ingredients. Cover and refrigerate 30 minutes. Drop by rounded tablespoonful onto a well greased cookie sheet. Bake at 325° 20 to 25 minutes or until lightly browned around the edges. Let stand 1 minute, then cool on wire rack.

Rose Anne Fielder
Georgia Beekeepers Association

Chewy Pecan Supreme Cookies

½ cup shortening
1½ cups packed brown sugar
2 eggs
1 teaspoon vanilla extract
1½ cups self-rising flour
1 cup crushed cornflakes
1½ cups chopped pecans

Cream shortening, brown sugar, eggs and vanilla. Add flour; mix well. Add cornflakes and pecans; mix well. Drop by teaspoonful on a cookie sheet treated with nonstick spray. Bake at 350° for 10 minutes.

Georgia Nut Butterscotch Cookies

1 cup butter
¾ cup sugar
¾ cup firmly packed brown sugar
2 eggs
1 teaspoon vanilla extract
2¼ cups all-purpose flour
1 teaspoon soda
⅛ teaspoon salt
½ cup chopped pecans
½ cup chopped peanuts

Cream butter and sugars in a bowl, mixing well. Add eggs and vanilla extract. Stir in remaining ingredients; mix well. Drop dough by teaspoons onto ungreased nonstick cookie sheets and bake at 375° for about 10 minutes. Cool and serve.

Georgia Goober Butter Cookies

1 can sweetened condensed milk
1 to 1¼ cups creamy peanut butter
1 egg, beaten
1 teaspoon vanilla extract
2 cups biscuit baking mix
½ cup sugar
Chopped Georgia peanuts

This recipe combines Georgia peanuts, sometimes referred to as "goobers" and peanut butter for a creamy and crunchy taste.

Beat condensed milk, peanut butter, egg and vanilla until smooth. Add biscuit mix; mix well. Refrigerate an hour or longer. Shape dough into 1-inch balls and roll in sugar. Place balls about 2 inches apart on ungreased baking sheet. Use a fork to press the balls flat and make in a criss-cross pattern in the dough. Press in a small amount of chopped peanuts. Bake at 350° about 15 minutes or until lightly browned; don't overcook.

Georgia Pecan Balls

1 stick (½ cup) butter
1 cup all-purpose flour
2 tablespoons sugar
1 teaspoon vanilla extract
½ teaspoon salt
1 cup finely chopped Georgia pecans
1 (16-ounce) box powdered sugar

In a bowl, combine all ingredients except powdered sugar. Mix with hands and roll into bite-sized balls. Place on ungreased cookie sheet and bake at 375° for 20 minutes. Remove from oven and allow cookies to cool for a few minutes. Roll each ball in powder sugar while still warm. You can add a dash of rum or bourbon to this recipe, if desired.

Fort Benning Quick Drop Cookies

1 cup sugar
1 cup brown sugar
½ cup butter
½ cup soy milk
2 tablespoons cocoa
¼ cup macadamia nut butter
3 cups oats
½ cup chopped macadamia nuts

Place sugar, brown sugar, butter, milk, and chocolate powder in a large saucepan. Bring to a boil over medium-high heat; boil 2 minutes, stirring constantly. Remove pan from heat; stir in macadamia nut butter until dissolved. Stir in oatmeal and nuts. Drop spoon-sized balls onto a wax-paper-lined cookie sheet, and place in the refrigerator to cool. Serve when set.

Peanut Butter and Mayhaw Jelly Cookies

½ cup packed brown sugar
¼ cup creamy peanut butter
¼ cup dark corn syrup
3 tablespoons butter or margarine, softened
1 large egg
2 teaspoons vanilla extract
1⅓ cups all-purpose flour
2 tablespoons cornstarch
½ teaspoon baking powder
¼ teaspoon baking soda
¼ teaspoon salt
¼ cup sugar
¼ cup mayhaw jelly

Beat brown sugar, peanut butter, corn syrup and butter on medium speed until well-blended. Add egg; beat well. Beat in vanilla. In separate bowl, combine flour, cornstarch, baking powder, baking soda, and salt; mix well. Add to peanut mixture beating well. Cover and freeze 30 minutes or until firm. Preheat oven to 375°. Shape dough into 24 balls; roll in granulated sugar. Place 1 inch apart on baking sheets coated with cooking spray. Press thumb into center of each cookie, leaving an indentation. Spoon about ½ teaspoon jelly into center of each cookie. Bake 12 minutes or until lightly browned. Cool 2 minutes on pans. Remove from pans, and cool completely on wire racks. Makes 2 dozen cookies.

National Mayhaw Festival
Colquitt • April

The National Mayhaw Festival is held at Spring Creek Recreation Park beginning with a barbecue, bake sale and live entertainment. The fun continues with a 5K race, one-mile fun walk and Main Street parade. Vendors will be selling arts, crafts, collectibles, and a variety of food including Mayhaw Jelly —"the best jelly in the world." With many special attractions and displays for all ages this popular festival is family fun at its best.

229.758.2400 • www.colquitt-georgia.com

Cornflake Raisin Cookies

½ stick butter
½ cup sugar
1 egg
1½ cups all-purpose flour
1 teaspoon baking powder
½ cup raisins
1 cup crushed cornflakes cereal

In a large bowl combine all ingredients except cereal. Mix well. Roll into small balls then roll in crushed cereal. Place cookies 2 inches apart on a parchment-lined baking sheet. Bake at 350° for 10 to 15 minutes. This cookies are great served warm.

Quick Fix Sugar Cookies

1 cup sugar
2 cups all-purpose flour
½ cup butter, softened
½ teaspoon baking soda
1 egg
½ teaspoon salt
2 tablespoons lemon juice

Mix all ingredients in a small bowl. Roll into small balls. Flatten on greased cookie sheet with the bottom of a glass dipped in sugar. Bake at 375° 8 to 10 minutes. Cool and serve.

Lotsa Chocolate, Chocolate Cookies

2 packages semi-sweet baking chocolate
¾ cup brown sugar
½ stick butter, softened
2 large eggs, beaten
1 teaspoon vanilla extract
½ cup all-purpose flour
¼ teaspoon baking powder
2 cups chopped nuts

Coarsely chop 1 package chocolate; set aside. Microwave remaining package chocolate to melt per directions on package. Add sugar, butter, eggs, vanilla, flour, baking powder, chopped chocolate and nuts; stir with spoon until well blended. Using a spoon, drop dough onto nonstick cookie sheets. Bake at 350° 13 to 14 minutes. Cool before serving.

Powdered Sugar Wedding Cookies

2 sticks butter, softened
2 cups powdered sugar, divided
2 cups all-purpose flour, divided
2 teaspoons vanilla extract
⅛ teaspoon salt
1 cup finely chopped pecans

Combine butter and ½ cup powdered sugar; beat with an electric mixer on medium until fluffy. Add 1 cup flour, vanilla and salt. Beat at low speed until well blended. Using a spoon, stir in remaining flour and pecans. Cover and refrigerate about an hour or until firm. Shape dough into 1-inch balls and place about 1 inch apart on a nonstick cookie sheet. Bake at 350° for 12 minutes until golden brown. Roll cookies in powdered sugar until coated well. Before serving, sprinkle with fresh powdered sugar.

Party Cookies

½ cup shortening
½ cup peanut butter
1 cup sugar
1 egg, beaten
2 tablespoons milk
1¼ cups all-purpose flour
½ teaspoon salt
½ teaspoon soda
2 (8-ounce) packages semi-sweet chocolate chips

My grandmother, Virginia Rice Cantrell, was born just outside Marietta, Georgia. This recipe was given to her in the early 1950s. My Mom made this special cookie when I was a child, and it is still my favorite cookie.

Mix shortening, peanut butter and sugar until creamy; add egg and milk. Sift flour, salt and soda. Add to shortening mixture to make a soft dough. Roll out on floured waxed paper to ¼-inch thick. Melt chocolate chips (I do this in the microwave) and spread on dough. Roll up and refrigerate at least 1 hour. Cut in ¼-inch slices and bake at 350° for 10 minutes or until light brown.

Holiday Time Tea Cookies

½ cup sugar
5 cups all-purpose flour
3½ teaspoons baking powder
1 large pinch salt
6 eggs
¼ cup milk
1 tablespoon grated orange peel
½ teaspoon vanilla extract
½ cup oil
½ tablespoon cinnamon

Icing

½ cup powdered sugar
Lemon juice

Combine sugar, flour, baking powder and salt until well mixed. Add eggs, milk, orange peel, vanilla, oil and cinnamon; mix well. Roll into small balls and place in candy or mini muffin paper cups. Bake at 350° approximately 20 minutes or until light brown. Cool while making icing. Combine sugar with drips of lemon juice, stirring, until thick like molasses. Spread over cookies.

Georgia

Kids Cream Cheese Cookies

1 stick (½ cup) unsalted butter, softened
2 (8-ounce) packages cream cheese, softened
1 tablespoon vanilla extract
2½ cups powdered sugar
1 box plain, large sugar cookies
   (NOT filled Oreo-style cookies)
 Raisins, pecans or chocolate chips

This cookie icing is perfect for kids to make then use on store-bought sugar cookies.

Cream butter and cream cheese. Blend in vanilla. Add powdered sugar and mix well. Spread over cookies. Allow children to make smiley faces or other designs on cookies using raisins, pecans or chocolate chips.

Dirty Birds Nest Cookies

2½ cups butterscotch chips
2 cups cornflakes
2 cups Chow Mein noodles
1 cup chocolate chips

Melt butterscotch chips. Stir in cornflakes and noodles. Gently fold in chocolate chips. Drop by spoonfuls onto wax paper. Cool to set before serving.

I first made this recipe when the Atlanta Falcons used Dirty Birds as their nickname. That name has faded some, but these cookies are still delicious!

Bake Sale No Bake Cookies

2 cups sugar
1 cup milk
½ cup butter
½ cup cocoa
Pinch salt
3 cups oatmeal
1 teaspoon vanilla extract
½ cup shredded coconut

In a saucepan, combine sugar, milk, butter and cocoa; bring to a full boil. Remove from heat; stir in salt, oatmeal, vanilla and coconut. Drop onto waxed paper by the spoonful and chill.

Susan Bowman
Ringgold, Georgia

Cookie Balls

1 package Oreos
1 (8-ounce) package cream cheese, softened
White candy-making chocolate for dipping

Crush cookies. (An easy way is to place in a zip-close bag and crush with fingers.) Mix in cream cheese. Form into balls and dip in melted chocolate. Place on waxed paper to set and harden. You can use any type of cream-filled sandwich cookie.

Crispy Rice Chocoscotch Squares

3 tablespoons butter
1 (10-ounce) package regular marshmallows (or 4 cups mini marshmallows)
6 cups crispy rice cereal
½ cup mini chocolate chips
½ cup mini butterscotch chips

In a saucepan, melt butter over low heat. Add marshmallows and stir until completely melted. Remove from heat and stir in cereal, chocolate and butterscotch chips. Stir until well coated. Press mixture evenly into a 9x13-inch pan coated with cooking spray. Cool and cut into squares.

Apple Crumb Squares

2 cups uncooked oatmeal
1½ cups all-purpose flour
¾ cup butter, melted
1 cup firmly packed brown sugar
1 teaspoon cinnamon
½ teaspoon salt
½ teaspoon baking soda
¼ teaspoon nutmeg, optional
1 cup applesauce
1/2 cup pecans, chopped

Preheat oven to 375°. Combine all ingredients, except applesauce and nuts, in a bowl. Mix until crumbly. Reserve 1 cup mixture. Press remaining mixture onto bottom of greased 9x13-inch baking pan. Bake 13 to 15 minutes; cool. Spread applesauce over partially baked crust and sprinkle with nuts. Sprinkle reserved 1 cup oatmeal mixture over filling. Bake an additional 13 to 15 minutes or until golden brown. Cool before cutting.

Box Cake
Bar Cookies

1 box yellow cake mix
⅓ cup butter, melted
1 large egg (or 2 small)
3 cups miniature marshmallows
1 package caramel chips
⅔ cup white corn syrup
½ stick butter
2 teaspoons vanilla extract
1 cup salted peanuts
2 cups puffed rice cereal
Melted candy chocolate, optional

Combine cake mix, butter and egg until well combined. Press into bottom of a treated 9x13-inch pan. Bake at 350° for 10 to 15 minutes. Remove from oven and carefully spread marshmallows over top; return to oven about 3 minutes. Remove from oven and cool. In a saucepan, heat caramel chips, corn syrup, butter and vanilla, stirring until smooth. Add peanuts and cereal. Spread over marshmallows. Drizzle with melted candy chocolate, if desired. Cool before cutting into bars.

Sorghum Festival

Blairsville • Second, third
and fourth week of October

This small-town celebration is centered around sorghum—a staple of early Georgia farmers. Sorghum has been a popular crop in North Georgia since the land was settled in the 1830s. Blairsville celebrates this early staple on the second, third and fourth weekends each October (the time the crop comes in). In 1995, the Sorghum Festival in Blairsville was designated Georgia's official sorghum festival.

706.745.4745 • www.sorghumfestival.com

Georgia

Topped Cake Mix Brownies

1 chocolate cake mix
2 large eggs
½ cup oil
6 ounces chocolate chips
½ cup broken Georgia pecans
Canned white icing

In a large bowl, thoroughly mix all ingredients except icing. Spoon into a 9x13-inch pan treated with nonstick spray. Bake 25 minutes at 350°. Remove from oven and allow to cool. Top with an even layer of icing.

Graham Cracker & Nut Brownies

25 graham cracker squares
6 ounces chocolate chips
1 can condensed milk
½ cup finely chopped peanuts or walnuts
Dash salt

Crush graham crackers into fine crumbs. (A food processor is helpful.) In a bowl, mix graham crackers with remaining ingredients, except icing. Spoon into a prepared 8-inch square pan. Bake at 350° about 25 minutes. Allow brownies to cool, cut into pieces, and serve.

Drunk as a Skunk Georgia Pecans

2 cups Georgia pecan halves
4 ounces whiskey
2 ounces brown sugar
½ tablespoon butter
1 tablespoon lemon juice
Sugar

In a skillet, cook pecans in whiskey, brown sugar, butter and lemon juice until caramelized. Cool and toss in a zip-close bag with sugar until well coated.

Macee's Hot Nuts 'n Stuff

⅔ stick butter
1 package taco seasoning
1 can mixed nuts
1 cup chex-style cereal
1 cup pretzel sticks

In a skillet, melt butter and stir in taco seasoning. Add nuts, cereal and pretzels. Mix well and spread on a cookie sheet. Bake at 200° about 10 minutes.

Macee Whitaker
Rossville, Georgia

Butter-Baked Georgia Pecans and Peanuts

⅔ stick butter
1 pound Georgia pecan halves
1 pound shelled Georgia raw peanuts
Salt to taste

Melt butter in a large skillet. Remove from heat and stir in pecans and peanuts to coat with butter. Spread evenly over cookie sheets and slow cook in oven at 200° about 10 minutes. Sprinkle with salt to taste.

Grannies Peanut Brittle

1 cup sugar
½ cup light corn syrup
½ cup water
1 cup shelled raw peanuts
1 teaspoon baking soda

In a large skillet, mix sugar, syrup and water together. Cook over medium-high heat, stirring regularly, heat until mixture thickens. Occasionally pull spoon out of mixture and look for drips that look like spider webs. When this happens, stir in peanuts. Continue to cook, stirring constantly, until mixture begins to brown. Remove from heat and stir in baking soda. Pour onto unbuttered foil as 1 big piece. Allow to cool then break into smaller pieces.

Strawberry Kisses

2 pounds whole strawberries
1 (8-ounce) package cream cheese
1 cup sugar
1 cup finely chopped pecans

Melt cream cheese in microwave for about 1 minute. Add sugar; stir until creamy. Hold strawberry by stem and dip into cream cheese mixture. Roll in pecans. Serve with toothpicks.

Rachel Horton
Georgia Strawberry Festival

This quick and easy recipe won 1st place in the Youth Division during the 2007 Georgia Strawberry Festival.

Georgia Strawberry Festival
Reynolds • Fourth weekend in April

The family-oriented Georgia Strawberry Festival salutes Georgia strawberry growers and their luscious product. The festival features great gospel entertainment, a leisurely dinner in the shady city park, artists, craftsmen, and Georgia strawberry growers with several varieties of the delicious berries and strawberry products for sampling and for sale. The crowd-pleasing Grand Parade is preceded by the Teddy Bear Parade led by festival mascot, Reynolds S. Berry, who leads the little ones and their teddy bears along the short route on foot or decorated tricycles, wagons or other conveyances. More fun includes a photography show, fine-art exhibit, old book sale, lawn mower races and the Statewide Strawberry Cook -Off. Family fun and sweet, delicious strawberries are the order of the day at the annual Georgia Strawberry Festival.

478.847.3435 • www.ga-strawberry.org

by Joseph Justice

Susan's Peanut Butter Fudge

1½ sticks butter
3 cups sugar
1 (7-ounce) can evaporated milk
1 bag peanut butter chips
1 (7-ounce) jar marshmallow cream
½ teaspoon vanilla extract

In a saucepan, bring butter, sugar and evaporated milk to a rolling boil. Boil, stirring constantly, for 5 minutes. Add peanut butter chips, marshmallow cream and vanilla. Stir until completely dissolved. Do not allow to stick to bottom. Quickly, but carefully pour mix into a pan and let cool at least 4 hours. Cut and serve.

Susan Bowman

In the Bag Fudge

¼ stick butter, softened
½ cup peanut butter
1 teaspoon vanilla extract
4 ounces cream cheese, softened
⅔ cup unsweetened cocoa powder
1 pound powdered sugar

An easy 10-minute fudge recipe.

Combine all ingredients in a large zip-close bag. Knead bag until everything is well mixed, about 8 to 10 minutes. Empty onto a sheet of foil and gently press down to form a flat fudge. Chill.

Susan Bowman

Creamy Orange White Chocolate Fudge

2 pounds white chocolate, melted
2 (8-ounce) packages cream cheese
6 cups powdered sugar
1½ tablespoons orange juice
1 tablespoon flour
1 cup chopped nuts, optional

Combine all ingredients; spoon into mini muffin/candy cups. Top with chopped nuts, if desired. Chill to set.

Party Popcorn

2 quarts popped popcorn
1 cup butter
2 cups brown sugar
½ cup white corn syrup
6 ounces salted peanuts
½ cup M&M plain candies

Remove unpopped kernels and set popcorn aside in a large bowl. In a microwave-safe bowl combine butter, brown sugar and corn syrup. Microwave 10 minutes on high. Check and stir as cooking. Remove container from microwave and stir in peanuts. Pour over popcorn and gently mix until well coated. Stir in M&Ms. Spread evenly onto cookie sheet lined with wax paper; cool.

Cakes

Ken's Apple Cake Supreme

3 cups all-purpose flour
1¼ cups sugar
½ cup firmly packed brown sugar
2 teaspoons cinnamon
1 teaspoon nutmeg
1 teaspoon salt
2 teaspoons baking soda
3 eggs
1 cup sour cream
2 teaspoons vanilla extract
1 cup vegetable oil
½ cup milk
4 cups chopped apples
1 cup chopped pecans

In large bowl, combine dry ingredients. Beat together eggs, sour cream, vanilla, oil and milk; add dry ingredients and beat another 2 minutes or until completely mixed. Fold in apples and pecans; stir until apples are coated. Pour batter into prepared bundt pan. Bake at 350° from 60 to 65 minutes or until a toothpick inserted in cake comes out clean (do not over-bake). Cool 10 minutes on wire rack; invert onto favorite cake plate and garnish with more apples if you like. We like it topped with whipped cream or vanilla ice cream. The apple cake is just fine by itself. ENJOY.

Kenneth Maye Jr.
Georgia Apple Festival

Georgia Apple Festival
Ellijay • October

The Ellijay Lions Club, the Gilmer County Chamber of Commerce, and the cities of Ellijay and East Ellijay invite everyone to come and enjoy the Georgia Apple Festival. There are over 300 vendors with handmade, hand-crafted items, as well as many on-site demonstrations of how selected types of crafts are made. Events include a parade and antique car show.

706.636.4500
www.georgiaapplefestival.org

Chocolate Apple Brownies Cake

1½ cups oil
2 cups sugar
4 eggs
2 teaspoons vanilla extract
3 cups sifted all-purpose flour
1 teaspoon salt
1 teaspoon baking soda
1 (21-ounce) box brownie mix
⅓ cup buttermilk
3 large apples, cut in small pieces
1 cup chopped pecans

Mix oil, sugar, eggs and vanilla at medium speed about 3 minutes. In a separate bowl, combine flour, salt and soda; add to oil mixture mixing on low speed. Add brownie mix and buttermilk; mix 1 minute. Add apples and pecans; beat at medium speed for 2 minutes. Pour in well-greased and floured tube pan. Bake at 325° for 1 hour 25 minutes. Cool in pan 5 to 10 minutes. Remove from pan. Pour sauce on top, if desired.

Sauce

½ stick melted butter
½ cup packed light brown sugar
2 teaspoons milk

Combine all sauce ingredients in a small saucepan over medium-high heat; bring to a boil. Reduce heat; cook 10 minutes. While hot, pour over cake.

Ann Futch
Georgia Apple Festival

Georgia Apple Topsy Turvy Cake

1½ sticks unsalted butter, softened (divided)
1¾ cups brown sugar, divided
3 to 4 large Georgia Granny Smith apples, peeled and sliced
1¼ cups chopped and toasted pecans, divided
2 large eggs
1½ cups all-purpose flour
1 teaspoon baking powder
2 teaspoons cinnamon
½ cup milk

In skillet, combine ½ stick butter, ¾ cup brown sugar and apples. Cook approximately 5 minutes, stirring often. Remove from heat and sprinkle with half of pecans. Mix remaining 1 stick butter and remaining 1 cup brown sugar until light and fluffy. Add eggs 1 at a time and mix well. Stir together dry ingredients; slowly add milk, mixing well. Stir in remaining pecans. Spoon batter evenly over apple mixture in skillet. Bake at 350° for 30 minutes. Cool in skillet 5 minutes before inverting on a serving plate. Top with ice cream and enjoy. Makes 8 servings

Ann Earley
Georgia Apple Festival

Tipsy Apple Cake

Topping

½ cup sugar
¼ cup Georgia apple cider
1 tablespoon lemon juice
1 tablespoon light butter
4 medium fresh Georgia apples (peeled, cored and each cut into 8 wedges)

Cake

¼ cup light butter, softened
⅔ cup sugar
1 teaspoon baking powder
2 tablespoons brandy
½ teaspoon apple pie spice
½ teaspoon baking soda
¼ teaspoon salt
2 large eggs
1¼ cups all-purpose flour
⅔ cup nonfat buttermilk
Whipping cream (optional)

Preheat oven to 350°. Coat a 9-inch round cake pan with nonstick spray. Mix sugar and cider in a large nonstick skillet; bring to a boil over medium-high heat. Boil until light honey color. Add lemon juice and butter; reduce heat to medium. Boil 1 minute, until light golden. Add apples, flat side down, and cook 8 minutes, turning apples after 4 minutes, until lightly caramelized and crisp-tender when pierced with a fork. Remove from heat; cool in skillet 5 minutes. Pour into prepared cake pan arranging apples in a concentric circle. Beat butter, sugar, baking powder, brandy, apple pie spice, baking soda and salt 2 minutes with a mixer. Beat in eggs, 1 at a time, until blended. Beat in flour and buttermilk until batter is smooth. Pour over apples spreading to edge of pan. Bake 40 to 45 minutes. Cool 10 minutes pan on wire rack. Invert onto a serving plate. Served warm or at room temperature. Top with whipping cream, if desired. Serves 8.

Ann Williams
Georgia Apple Festival

Coconut Peach Upside-Down Cake

6 tablespoons butter
⅔ cup brown sugar
1 tablespoon light corn syrup
1⅓ cups flaked coconut
1 (16-ounce) can peach slices, drained
1 cup sifted all-purpose flour (sift before measuring)
¾ cup sugar
1¼ teaspoons baking powder
¼ teaspoon salt
¼ cup shortening
1 egg
½ cup milk
½ teaspoon vanilla extract

Preheat oven to 375°. Melt butter in an 8-inch square baking pan in oven. Stir in brown sugar, corn syrup and coconut. Arrange peaches over coconut. Into a medium mixing bowl, sift together the sifted flour, sugar, baking powder and salt. Add remaining ingredients and blend on low speed of electric mixer. Increase mixer speed to medium and beat 2 minutes. Spread batter over peaches. Bake at 375° for 40 minutes, or until a wooden pick or cake tester inserted in center comes out clean. Cool in pan for a minute or 2 before turning out onto serving plate. Serve warm with whipped topping or ice cream, if desired.

Cordele-Crisp County Watermelon Cake

1 white cake mix
1⅓ cups cubed seedless Watermelon
1 package mixed-fruit gelatin
3 egg whites
1 tablespoon oil

Preheat oven to 350°. Grease and flour bundt pan. In large bowl, combine dry cake mix, cubed watermelon, dry gelatin powder, egg whites and oil. Beat until smooth. Pour into prepared pan and bake about 35 minutes or until a toothpick inserted comes out clean. Cool on a rack and frost with your favorite icing.

Recipe by Chef and the Fatman
Compliments of Watermelon Days Festival

Lemon Poppy Seed Bundt Cake

1 white cake mix
1 cup mayonnaise
3 large eggs, beaten
2 tablespoons poppy seeds
2 teaspoons grated lemon rind
Juice of 1 lemon, divided
1 cup powdered sugar

Preheat oven to 350°. Combine dry cake mix, mayonnaise, eggs, poppy seeds, lemon rind, 4 tablespoons lemon juice and ⅔ cup water; beat until batter is smooth. Pour into a greased and floured 12-cup Bundt pan. Bake 35 to 40 minutes or until a toothpick inserted in the center comes out clean. Cool 15 to 20 minutes. Drizzle with powdered sugar mixed with 2 tablespoons lemon juice. Serves 12.

Fresh Apple Cake with Caramel Glaze

Cake

1 cup light brown sugar
1 cup sugar
1½ cups vegetable oil
3 eggs
3 cups all-purpose flour
1 teaspoon baking soda
2 teaspoons ground cinnamon
½ teaspoon ground nutmeg
½ teaspoon salt
5 medium to large apples, peeled and diced (any tart, firm, Georgia-grown apple will do)
½ cup Georgia-grown pecans, chopped
2 teaspoons vanilla extract

1st place winner
Georgia Apple Festival 2007

Preheat oven to 350°. Spray a 9x13-inch baking pan with nonstick spray. In a mixing bowl, beat both sugars and oil until well-blended. Add eggs 1 at a time, beating well after each. Sift together flour, baking soda, cinnamon, nutmeg and salt. Gradually add flour mixture to sugar and eggs. Mix just until well blended. Stir in apples, pecans and vanilla. Pour into baking pan. Bake 50 to 75 minutes, until toothpick inserted in the center comes out clean. Cool in pan while preparing glaze.

Glaze

4 tablespoons (½ stick) butter
¼ cup sugar
¼ cup light brown sugar
Pinch salt
½ cup heavy cream (whipping cream)

In a saucepan, melt butter. Add both sugars and salt. Stir until well-blended and cook over medium-low heat for 2 minutes. Stir in cream and boil for 2 minutes, stirring constantly. Remove from heat. With a skewer or toothpick, poke holes all over top of warm cake. Pour glaze over surface. Cool before serving.

Teresa Standfield • Georgia Apple Festival

Big Red Apple Festival
Cornelia • First Saturday in October

Because Cornelia is home to the Big Red Apple Monument, it is also host of The Big Red Apple Festival—an outdoor event held in Downtown Cornelia in October so that visitors can enjoy the fall colors and cooler days. This well-attended festival turns downtown Cornelia into a venue for artists, crafters, food vendors and more. Also featured are children's activities, live entertainment, chili cook-off, apple bake-off, and more.

706.778.8585 • www.corneliageorgia.org

Pineapple Colada Cake

Cake
3½ cups all-purpose flour
1½ cups sugar
2 teaspoons baking soda
¼ teaspoon salt
3 eggs
1 (20-ounce) can crushed pineapple with juice
½ cup shredded coconut
½ cup liquid piña colada mix (non-alcoholic)

Icing
¾ cup sugar
¾ cup evaporated milk
½ pound (2 sticks) butter
1 cup chopped pecans
1 cup flaked coconut

In a large bowl, combine flour, sugar, baking soda, salt, eggs, pineapple with half the juice and piña colada mix. Stir until well blended. Pour batter into a prepared 9x13-inch pan and bake at 350° for 35 minutes or until done. Check with a toothpick. While cake cooks, combine sugar, milk, butter, pecans and coconut in a saucepan. Bring to a boil, stirring constantly. As soon as mixture boils, reduce heat and stir for about 1 minute. Pour over cake as soon as it comes out of oven. Allow to cool slightly before serving.

Ashton's "Double Secret" UGA Chocolate Cake

1 cup mayonnaise (Ashton's "Double Secret" ingredient)
1 cup sugar
1 teaspoon vanilla extract
2 teaspoons baking soda
2 cups flour
1 cup water
5 tablespoons cocoa
1 can cherry icing

This is young Ashton's cake recipe. Ashton's daddy was born in Georgia and her Mom Kathryn is a certified Georgia Bulldog fan!

Mix all ingredients, except cherry icing. Pour into a greased and floured 9x13-inch pan. (You can make this as a layer cake using 2 round pans, but you'll probably need 2 cans of icing). Bake at 350° for 30 to 35 minutes or until a toothpick comes out clean; cool. Frost with cherry icing. This makes a very moist cake, that will have all your friends asking for the recipe.

Lil' Ashton "My Daddy was Born in Georgia" Spencer

Chocolate Sheet Cake

2 cups sugar
2 cups all-purpose flour
½ teaspoon salt
1 cup water
½ cup oil
1 stick (½ cup) butter or margarine
3 tablespoons cocoa
½ cup buttermilk
1 teaspoon baking soda
2 eggs, beaten
1 teaspoon vanilla extract

Mix sugar, flour and salt in large mixing bowl. In large boiler, heat water, oil, butter and cocoa over medium-high heat just until butter melts. Pour over dry mixture; mix. Combine buttermilk and soda; add to batter and mix well. Combine eggs and vanilla; add to batter and mix well. Pour into a 9x13-inch glass baking dish treated with nonstick spray. Bake at 350° for 30 minutes. Cool before icing.

Icing

1 box powdered sugar
3 tablespoons cocoa
1 stick (½ cup) butter or margarine, softened
6 tablespoons buttermilk
1 teaspoon vanilla extract

Combine all ingredients in large boiler and cook until butter has melted. Beat with spoon until smooth and a spreading consistency. Spread over cooled cake.

Georgia Pecan Marbled Cake

Cake

1 box white cake mix
4 eggs
⅔ cup vegetable oil
⅓ cup water
1 (8-ounce) carton sour cream (not fat-free)

Marbling

⅔ cup brown sugar
½ tablespoon ground cinnamon
1 cup chopped Georgia pecans
½ cup melted butter

Topping

1 cup powdered sugar
2 tablespoons milk
½ teaspoon vanilla extract
1 tablespoon maple syrup

In a large bowl, combine cake ingredients and beat until smooth. Pour half the batter into a prepared 9x13-inch baking pan. Combine marbling ingredients; pour over batter in pan. Pour remaining cake batter over marbling mixture. Use a knife or fork to gently swirl the batters to create marbled look. Bake in a 350° oven about 30 minutes. While cake is cooking, combine topping ingredients in a bowl until smooth. When cake is done spread topping evenly over top while still hot. Top with additional pecans if desired. Cool before cutting.

Easy Cinnamon Coffee Cake

1 tube crescent rolls
1 teaspoon vanilla extract
¾ cup sugar, divided
1 egg yolk, beaten
1 (8-ounce) package cream cheese, softened
1 teaspoon cinnamon
¼ cup chopped pecans, optional

Spray an 8x8-inch pan with nonstick spray. Lay ½ crescent rolls flat in bottom of pan. Combine ½ cup sugar, egg yolk, and cream cheese; spoon over crescent rolls in pan. Top with remaining crescent rolls. Combine remaining ¼ cup sugar, cinnamon, and pecans; sprinkle over top. Bake 30 to 35 minutes at 350° or until dough is cooked through and lightly browned. Serves 6 to 8.

Mercer Williams House
Savannah

Laszlo • shutterstock.com

Sweet Potato Cake

1 cup vegetable oil
2 cups sugar
4 eggs
1½ cups shredded sweet potato
¼ cup hot water
1 teaspoon vanilla extract
1½ cups self-rising flour
1 teaspoon cinnamon
1 cup chopped walnuts

In a mixing bowl, beat oil and sugar. Add eggs 1 at a time, beating well after each. Add sweet potato, water and vanilla; mix well. Combine flour and cinnamon; add to potato mixture. Stir in walnuts. Pour into 3 baking pans and bake 25 to 30 minutes at 350°.

Cream Cheese Frosting

1 stick (½ cup) margarine
1 (8-ounce) package cream cheese
1 (16-ounce) box powdered sugar
1 teaspoon vanilla extract
1 cup nuts

Cream margarine and cream cheese. Add sugar, vanilla and nuts. Spread between cooled layers over top of cake.

Edna Wright, 2nd Place 2005
Miss Georgia Sweet Potato Pageant

Pumpkin Festival
Stone Mountain • weekends in October

Stone Mountain Park's Pumpkin Festival offers fall fun for the whole family. Taking place in the 1870's town of Crossroads, guests will soak in the fall décor while enjoying the many activities and entertainment for all ages. Whether it's painting pumpkins, trying to find their way through Farmer Brown's A MAZE ing Adventure or participating in the pumpkin pie eating contests, guests are sure to discover excitement around every corner. Additionally, Stone Mountain Park's Pumpkin Festival activities and entertainment include: Corney Island, Mad Science Show, the South's largest pumpkin tree, pumpkin patch and a live train show.

770.498.5600
www.stonemountainpark.com

Sweet Potato Torte

1 yellow cake mix
1½ baked sweet potatoes, divided
½ cup milk
⅓ cup vegetable oil
4 eggs
1½ teaspoons cinnamon, divided
¼ teaspoon nutmeg
1 (8-ounce) package cream cheese
1 cup powdered sugar
1 (16-ounce) carton whipped topping
¼ cup caramel ice cream topping
⅓ cup toasted chopped pecans

Combine cake mix, 1 cup sweet potato, milk, oil, eggs, 1 teaspoon cinnamon and ¼ teaspoon nutmeg on low speed until mixed. Beat on medium for 2 minutes. Pour into 4 greased and floured 9-inch round baking pans. Bake at 350° 25 to 30 minutes. Cool 10 minutes before removing pans to wire racks. Cool completely. Beat cream cheese, sugar, remaining sweet potato and ½ teaspoon cinnamon until smooth. Fold in whipped topping. Place 1 cake layer on a plate, spread with ¼ of the filling. Repeat using all layers. Top with caramel topping and pecans. Chill.

Lisa Martin, 1st Place
Miss Georgia Sweet Potato Pageant

Buttermilk Carrot Cake

⅔ cup all-purpose flour
1 pound carrots, peeled and grated
1 cup buttermilk
3 large eggs, beaten
2 teaspoons baking soda
2½ teaspoons cinnamon
½ teaspoon salt
½ teaspoon ground nutmeg
¼ teaspoon ground ginger
1 cup sugar
1¼ cups brown sugar
¾ cup vegetable oil
1½ teaspoons vanilla extract
1 can crushed pineapple, drained
1 cup chopped Georgia pecans
1 cup coconut
½ cup raisins

Frosting

½ cup butter, softened
1 (8-ounce) cream cheese, softened
1 (16-ounce) package powdered sugar
1 teaspoon vanilla extract

Mix all cake ingredients in a large bowl. Pour into 2 round prepared cake pans and bake in a 350° oven for 35 minutes or until a toothpick inserted in center comes out clean. Cool and remove from pans. While cake cools, combine butter and cream cheese in a large mixing bowl; beat until light and fluffy. Add sugar and vanilla while continuing to mix. Spread evenly on cake.

Iced Blueberry Cupcakes

Cupcakes

1½ cups blueberries
1½ cups sugar, divided
10 eggs, beaten
1 cup plus 2 tablespoons cake flour
1¼ teaspoons cream of tartar
½ teaspoon salt
1 teaspoon vanilla extract
2 teaspoons orange juice

Icing

1 cup powdered sugar
3 tablespoons lemon juice
1 teaspoon melted butter

Rinse blueberries, sprinkle with ½ cup sugar, and set aside. Combine remaining 1 cup sugar with remaining cupcake ingredients; mix well to form a smooth batter. Stir in blueberries; mix well. Using a muffin tin with paper-lined muffin cups fill each cup about ¾ full. Bake at 375° about 15 minutes. Remove from oven. While cupcakes cool, combine powder sugar, lemon juice and melted butter. Spread icing on cooled cupcakes.

Picnic Red Velvet Cupcakes

1 box strawberry cake mix
   plus ingredients for preparing per directions
1 single-serving package hot chocolate mix
1 can cream cheese or white icing
Chopped peanuts or pecans

Prepare cake mix as directed on box; stir in dry hot chocolate mix. Cook as directed on box using paper-lined muffin tins. Cool; top with icing and sprinkle with chopped nuts.

St. Simons Lighthouse
St. Simons Island

Photograph courtesy of the Coastal Georgia Historical Society

Georgia

Red Velvet Cake

3 tablespoons cocoa
2 (1-ounce) bottles red food coloring
½ cup shortening
1½ cups sugar
2 eggs
2¼ cups all-purpose flour
½ teaspoon salt
1 cup buttermilk
1 teaspoon vanilla extract
1 teaspoon almond extract
1 teaspoon baking soda
1 tablespoon vinegar

Mix cocoa and food coloring. Add shortening, sugar and eggs; cream well. Sift together flour and salt. Add sifted dry ingredients to shortening mixture alternately with buttermilk. Blend in vanilla and almond flavorings. In a small bowl, stir soda into vinegar then quickly stir into batter. Pour into 2 or 3 (9-inch) cake pans. Bake at 375° 25 minutes or until done. Cool; frost with Ice Cream Frosting.

Ice Cream Frosting

4½ tablespoons all-purpose flour
1 cup milk
½ pound (2 sticks) margarine or butter
1 cup powdered sugar
1 teaspoon vanilla extract

In a small saucepan, whisk together flour and milk. Cook over low heat, whisking well to prevent lumping, until thick. Set aside to cool. Cream margarine and continue to beat 4 minutes; add powdered sugar and beat 4 minutes longer. Add cooled flour paste and vanilla. Beat 4 to 5 minutes. Spread on cooled cake.

Evelyn Hunsucker
St. Simon, Georgia

Popcorn Cake

1 (16-ounce) bag miniature marshmallows
1 stick (½ cup) butter
3 packages microwave popcorn, popped with unpopped kernels removed
1 (16-ounce) bag plain M&Ms
1 (8-ounce) container cocktail peanuts

Melt marshmallows and butter over low heat. Combine popped popcorn, M&Ms, and peanuts in a large bowl. Pour melted marshmallows over and stir quickly to coat. Press into buttered bundt pan. Cover with aluminum foil and let rest at least 1 hour before inverting onto serving dish. Serve at room temperature.

Pies & Other Desserts

Peanut Parfait Pie

2 (9-inch) pie shells, baked and cooled
1 (8-ounce) package cream cheese, softened
1 (14-ounce) can sweetened condensed milk
1 (16-ounce) carton whipped topping
1 (12-ounce) jar hot fudge ice cream topping
2 cups dry roasted peanuts

Combine cream cheese and condensed milk with electric mixer until smooth; fold in whipped topping by hand. Spread ¼ mixture into each pie shell. Warm topping in microwave just until warm enough to pour. Drizzle ¼ on each pie; cover with peanuts. Repeat cream cheese layer; drizzle with remaining fudge topping. Cover and freeze overnight (or at least 4 hours).

Mix & Chill Peanut Butter Pie

⅓ cup creamy peanut butter
1 cup powdered sugar
1 (4-ounce) package cream cheese, softened
1 (8-ounce) container Cool Whip
1 graham cracker crust
Chopped peanuts

Combine peanut butter, powdered sugar, cream cheese and Cool Whip. Spread filling into pie crust; top with nuts. Refrigerate 1½ hours or longer. Top with additional Cool Whip before serving, if desired. For a twist, toss in a handful of chocolate chips when making the filling.

Cordele-Crisp County Watermelon Chiffon Pie Recipe

2 cups puréed watermelon
½ cup powdered sugar
2 tablespoons unflavored gelatin
¼ cup cold water
¾ cup boiling water
1 tablespoon lemon juice
2 egg whites, stiffly-beaten
1 cup whipping cream, whipped
1 graham cracker crust
Whipped cream to garnish

Purée watermelon to measure 2 cups; stir in powered sugar and set aside. Soften unflavored gelatin in cold water. Add boiling water; stir to dissolve. Add lemon juice and puréed watermelon. Refrigerate until mixture begins to thicken. Fold in egg whites and 1 cup whipped cream. Pour into pie shell and refrigerate until firm. Garnish with more whipped cream. Makes 1 (10-inch) or 2 (8-inch) pies. Yields 10 servings.

Watermelon Days Festival

Sweet Potato Dream Pie

1 (4-ounce) package cream cheese
1 (8-ounce) carton whipped topping, divided
1 cup powdered sugar
1 cup cooked and mashed sweet potatoes
½ teaspoon ground cinnamon
1 teaspoon vanilla extract
1 graham cracker crust
Chopped pecans

A delicious no-bake pie.

In a mixing bowl, combine cream cheese, 1 cup whipped topping and powdered sugar. Mix until smooth. Add sweet potatoes, cinnamon and vanilla; mix until smooth. Pour into pie shell. Top with remaining whipped topping and garnish with pecans.

Lisa Martin, 1st Place 2005
Miss Georgia Sweet Potato Pageant

Chocolate Lovers Pudding Pie

1 cup chocolate chips, divided
1 graham cracker pie crust
2 boxes instant chocolate pudding plus milk to prepare per directions on box
1 (4-ounce) package cream cheese, softened
Whipped topping
Chocolate syrup or hard shell

Sprinkle ½ cup chocolate chips in pie crust. Prepare pudding per directions for pie filling. Combine with cream cheese; mix well. Spoon gently over chocolate chips in pie crust. Top with remaining chocolate chips. Chill at least 1 hour before serving. Top slices with whipped cream and chocolate syrup.

Big Mama's Deep-Dish Strawberry-Cobbler Pie with Strawberry Whipped Cream

Deep-Dish Strawberry-Cobbler Pie

2 cups sugar
2 to 4 tablespoons cornstarch
8 cups sliced fresh strawberries
1 teaspoon vanilla extract
1 teaspoon strawberry extract
⅓ cup butter
1 double-crust pastry recipe

Combine first 3 ingredients in a Dutch oven; set aside until syrup forms. Bring to a boil. Reduce heat to low and cook 10 minutes or until tender. Remove from heat; add extracts and butter. Stirring until butter melts. Roll ⅓ pastry to ⅛-inch thickness on a slightly floured surface. Cut into a 9-inch circle; set aside. Roll another ⅓ pastry to cover your 9-inch pie plate; trim edges, fold under and flute as desired. Spoon half of strawberries into pie crust. Top with reserved pastry circle. Bake at 475° for 12 minutes or until lightly browned. Spoon remaining strawberries over baked pastry circle. Roll remaining pastry to ⅛-inch thickness and cut into 1-inch strips. Arrange in a lattice design over strawberries. Bake an additional 15 to 18 minutes or until golden brown. Garnish with Strawberry Whipped Cream, sprinkle with toasted almond slices and strawberries. Serve hot or cold.

Strawberry Whipped Cream

1 (8-ounce) carton heavy whipping cream
3 to 4 tablespoons powdered sugar, sifted
¼ cup strawberries, finely chopped
½ teaspoon strawberry extract

Place whipping cream in a chilled bowl. Beat on high until foamy. Add sugar 1 tablespoon at a time to get desired sweetness. Beat until firm peaks form. Fold in strawberries and extract.

Recipe by Jean Jackson, 1st place 2007 Pie Division
Submitted by Georgia Strawberry Festival

Cookies & Cream Strawberry Pie

1 cup sliced strawberries
½ cup sugar
1½ tablespoons cornstarch
¼ teaspoon baking powder
½ tablespoon orange juice
1½ cups crushed Oreo cookies
⅓ cup butter, melted
1 (4-ounce) carton Welch's Lemon Breeze frozen concentrate juice, thawed
1 (14-ounce) can sweetened condensed milk
1 (8-ounce) carton Cool Whip

Mash strawberries; combine with sugar, cornstarch and baking powder in a saucepan. Bring to a boil over medium heat. Lower heat to medium low and cook until thick. Stir in orange juice; cool. Preheat oven to 350°. Combine Oreo crumbs and melted butter; press into a deep-dish pie plate. Bake 6 minutes; cool. Combine lemon breeze concentrate, condensed milk and Cool Whip; chill. To assemble pie, spread Cool Whip mixture into bottom and up sides of cookie crust. Fill the center with the cooked and cooled strawberry filling. Chill until ready to serve.

Rhonda Hitch, 3rd place Pie Division
Georgia Strawberry Festival

Sweet Georgia Brown Pecan Pie

3 eggs, beaten
1 cup sugar
1 cup light or dark corn syrup
1 teaspoon vanilla extract
3 tablespoons butter, melted and cooled
1½ cups chopped pecans
1 (9-inch) unbaked pie crust

I love pecan pie! Here is one of my favorites which features Georgia-grown pecans.

Combine eggs, sugar, corn syrup, vanilla and melted butter. Stir in pecans a handful at a time. Pour into unbaked pie crust. Bake at 350° for 45 to 55 minutes. Cool before slicing.

Brown Sugar Pie

½ cup all-purpose flour
2 cups packed brown sugar
1 (12-ounce) can evaporated milk
4 tablespoons butter
½ teaspoon salt
1 teaspoon vanilla extract
1 unbaked pie shell

Preheat oven to 400°. Combine all ingredients, except pie shell, in a saucepan; cook over medium heat until boiling. Pour into unbaked pie shell. Reduce oven to 350° and bake 25 minutes or until set.

Fresh-Baked Homestyle Georgia Peach Pie

2 ready-to-bake pie crusts
2 cups chopped Georgia peaches
1 cup sugar
2 tablespoons water
¼ cup all-purpose flour
¼ teaspoon cinnamon
¼ teaspoon nutmeg
⅛ teaspoon allspice
⅛ teaspoon ground ginger
2 tablespoons butter, cut into ¼-inch pieces

Preheat oven to 425°. Fit 1 pie crust to a prepared pie plate. Bake 5 minutes. Remove from oven; allow to cool while cooking filling. (When bottom crust is cooked, lower oven temperature to 350°.) In a saucepan, combine Georgia peaches, sugar, water, flour, cinnamon, nutmeg, allspice, and ginger; simmer 10 minutes or until thickened. Pour into prepared crust to about ¾ full. Dot with butter pieces. Top with remaining pie crust and crimp edges to close. Bake at 350° for 30 to 40 minutes.

Peach Custard Pie

1 egg, beaten
½ cup milk
½ cup white Karo (corn syrup)
¼ cup melted butter
¼ cup sugar
1 teaspoon vanilla extract

½ cup self-rising flour
2½ cups peaches
1 cup shredded coconut
Cinnamon
½ cup chopped pecans

Preheat oven to 350°. Combine egg, milk, syrup, butter, sugar, vanilla and flour in a large bowl. Stir in peaches and coconut. Pour into a greased and floured pie pan. Sprinkle with cinnamon to taste and top with pecans. Bake 40 to 50 minutes or until set. Let stand 30 minutes to 1 hour before cutting. (This is very important, otherwise the pie will run when cut.)

Pecan Meringue Peach Pie

3 egg whites
1 cup sugar
14 saltine crackers, finely crushed
1 teaspoon vanilla extract
¼ teaspoon baking powder
½ cup chopped pecans
7 Georgia peaches, peeled and sliced
2 cups Cool Whip

Preheat oven to 325°. Whip egg whites until stiff. Gradually sprinkle in sugar, while continuing to whip egg whites to stiff peaks. Fold in saltines, vanilla, baking powder and pecans. Spread evenly into an ungreased 9-inch deep-dish pie plate. Bake 30 minutes or until a toothpick inserted into the center comes out clean. Cool (crust will puff and crack as it cools). When crust is completely cool, arrange sliced peaches over top. Top with Cool Whip just before serving.

World's Largest Peach Cobbler

75 gallons sliced Georgia peaches
150 pounds self-rising flour
150 pounds sugar
32 gallons milk
90 pounds butter

Divide self-rising flour, sugar and milk into six equal parts; pour into six clean trashcans. Mix thoroughly with clean boat paddle. Sizzle 90 pounds butter in a 5-foot x 11-foot baking pan 6 inches deep. Pour in batter then add 75 gallons sliced peaches. Bake at 350° about 4 hours until golden brown. If you can't get fresh or fresh frozen peaches, you better be prepared to open a lot of giant cans of peaches.

Georgia Peach Festival

Georgia Peach Festival
Byron & Fort Valley • June

The purpose of the Peach Festival is to honor peach growers for their contribution to our state's economy and to the food industry nationwide. Featuring concerts, a parade, food vendors, arts & craft exhibits, music and dancing, fireworks, and the world's largest peach cobbler, the Peach Festival holds the honor of being the only state-sanctioned food festival in Georgia.

toll-free 1.87.PEACHES
www.worldslargestpeachcobbler.com

Caroline Klapper • bigstockphoto.com

Quick and Easy Peach Cobbler

1 cup self-rising flour
1 cup sugar
1 cup milk
1 stick (½ cup) butter
2 cups sliced fresh Georgia peaches

Preheat oven to 350°. Mix together flour, sugar and milk. Melt butter in microwave oven and pour into disposable baking pan. While butter is still hot, add batter and top with fresh peaches. Bake 25 to 30 minutes until golden brown. If you can't get fresh or fresh frozen peaches, use 1 large can of peaches.

Georgia Peach Festival

FiFi's Crockpot Peach Cobbler

1 (29-ounce) can sliced peaches, undrained
1 stick (½ cup) butter
1¾ cup sugar
1½ teaspoons cinnamon
1 package large refrigerated biscuits, cooked and crumbled
   (or left-over biscuits)

Cook peaches with juice, butter, sugar and cinnamon in a crockpot on high until butter melts; stir often. Add biscuits and mix well. Reduce heat to low and simmer 2 hours, stirring occasionally. Delicious served warm or cold.

Georgia Peach Buckle

2 pounds (6 to 8 medium) Georgia peaches, peeled and sliced thin
1 tablespoon lemon juice
¾ cup sugar, divided
4 tablespoons butter, softened
1 teaspoon vanilla extract
1 egg, beaten
1 cup self-rising flour
⅓ cup milk

A rich and delicious dessert that is well worth the effort.

Preheat oven to 375°. Toss peaches with lemon juice and ¼ cup sugar; set aside. Cream butter with remaining ½ cup sugar; add vanilla and egg. Mix well. Add small amounts of flour and milk alternately to creamed mixture, mixing well after each addition. Pour into a greased 10-inch baking disk. Spoon peaches over batter.

Topping

⅓ cup sugar
⅓ cup flour
¼ cup butter

Combine all ingredients to form coarse crumbs; sprinkle over fruit. Bake 40 to 50 minutes or until golden brown. Serve warm. Delicious served with ice cream or whipped cream. Serves 8 to 10.

Easy Peach Crisp

2 (16-ounce) cans peach pie filling
1 box yellow cake mix
2 sticks butter
1 cup chopped pecans

Preheat oven to 350°. Pour both cans of pie filling into a 9x13-inch baking dish. Sprinkle dry cake mix over pie filling; dot with slices of butter using both sticks. Sprinkle chopped nuts on top. Bake 45 to 55 minutes. Delicious served with ice cream or whipped topping.

Apple Crisp

½ cup water
½ cup sugar
1 teaspoon cinnamon
4 cups diced apples (about 4 nice-sized apples;
    Jonathan apples are good)
1 cup brown sugar
1 cup all-purpose flour
½ cup butter

Stir water, sugar and cinnamon together in bottom of 7x11-inch baking dish. Stir in apples. Mix brown sugar, flour and butter with fingers until crumbly; sprinkle on top. Bake 35 minutes at 350°; serve warm.

Blueberry Dumplings

2½ cups fresh or frozen blueberries
2 tablespoons plus 1½ cups sugar, divided
2 packages crescent rolls
1¾ cups water
1½ sticks butter
1 teaspoon cornstarch

Sprinkle blueberries with 2 tablespoons sugar. Separate crescent rolls and press each into circle. Put 1 heaping tablespoon blueberries on each section; pinch together. Arrange dumplings, pinched side down, in 9x13-inch baking dish. Mix 1½ cups sugar, water, butter and cornstarch in a saucepan. Bring to boil. Pour over dumplings. Bake at 350° approximately 30 minutes. Delicious served plain or with vanilla ice cream.

National Blueberry Festival

Georgia Blueberry Festival
Alma • June

The annual Georgia Blueberry Festival celebrates Alma/Bacon County as "Georgia's Blueberry Capital". This fun, family-oriented event has arts and crafts, entertainment, antique cars and tractors, games, rides, paintings, ceramics, wood products and many other activities. The event is free to the public.

912.632.5859 • www.abcchamber.org

Gloria's Mouth-Watering 40-Minute Cobbler

1 stick (½ cup) margarine
1 cup all-purpose flour
½ teaspoon salt
1 teaspoon baking powder
1 cup sugar
1 cup milk
1 can favorite fruit filling (blueberry, peach and cherry are Georgia favorites)

A quick and easy recipe that will have everyone coming back for seconds.

Preheat oven to 350°. Melt margarine in deep oven-safe skillet. Mix flour, salt, baking powder, and sugar in mixing bowl. Add milk; mix well. Pour into melted butter in skillet; stir to mix lightly. Add fruit filling; mix lightly. Cook in oven 20 to 35 minutes, until edges and top are golden brown.

Bruce and Gloria Spencer
Rossville, Georgia

Decadent Black Forest Dessert

1 cup all-purpose flour
2 tablespoons sugar
½ cup butter
½ cup flaked coconut
½ cup chopped walnuts, lightly toasted for 10 minutes at 350°
1 (8-ounce) package cream cheese, softened
1 cup powdered sugar
1 (8-ounce) carton whipped topping, divided
1 (21-ounce) can cherry pie filling
1½ cups semisweet chocolate chips
2½ cups cold milk
2 (3.4-ounce) packages instant vanilla pudding

Combine flour and sugar; cut in butter until crumbly. Stir in coconut and walnuts; press into a greased 9x13-inch glass baking dish. Bake 15 to 20 minutes at 350° or until crust is lightly browned. Cool. Beat cream cheese until fluffy; add powdered sugar and continue to beat until smooth. Fold in 1 cup whipped topping; spread over crust. Top with pie filling, cover, and place in refrigerator while you complete the next step. Melt chocolate chips in microwave; stir until smooth. Whisk cold milk and pudding until thick (about 2 minutes). Combine chocolate and pudding. Remove pan from fridge and cover pie filling with chocolate mixture. Spread remaining whipped topping over top. Chill at least 2 hours or overnight.

Ice Cream Cookie Dessert

1 (18-ounce) package Oreos, crushed (divided)
¼ cup butter, melted
½ gallon vanilla ice cream, softened
1 (16-ounce) jar hot fudge ice cream topping
1 (8-ounce) carton whipped topping

Reserve ½ cup cookie crumbs. Combine remaining cookie crumbs with melted butter. Press into bottom of a greased 9x13-inch glass baking dish. Spread with softened ice cream. Cover and freeze at least 2 hours. Warm fudge ice cream topping and drizzle over ice cream; cover and freeze 1 hour longer. Spread whipped topping over fudge layer and sprinkle with reserved cookie crumbs. Cover and freeze 2 hours or until firm. Remove from freezer 5 to 10 minutes before serving. Serves 12.

Homemade Peach Ice Cream

3 cups sugar, plus more for peaches
4 eggs, beaten
1 gallon milk, divided
1 tablespoon vanilla extract
4 to 6 medium-sized Georgia peaches, peeled and halved
1 can sweetened condensed milk
2 (12-ounce) cans evaporated milk
Ice
Rock salt

Combine 3 cups sugar, eggs, 4 cups milk and vanilla in a saucepan; cook over medium-high heat, stirring very frequently, until slightly thickened. Remove from heat and cool. While cooling, blend peaches and sugar to taste in a blender until smooth. Add to cooked mixture along with condensed milk and evaporated milk. Pour into a 6-quart ice cream maker and add more milk to reach fill line. Freeze according to manufacturer's directions using ice and rock salt.

Grilled Banana Split

Under-ripe bananas (1 for each guest)
Milk chocolate candy bars (with nuts) broken into small pieces
Miniature marshmallows

There is no need to use precise measurements as it's easy to adjust the amount of bananas and chocolate candy to match your guest list.

Hold banana with peeling, on a cutting board with curved side up. Using a sharp knife, slit the banana from end to end; cut deep but leave the bottom peeling intact. Force the slit open (without breaking peel) and stuff with pieces of chocolate and marshmallows. The amount you put into each banana is determined by how much can be stuffed inside without breaking the peel. Wrap bananas in foil, rolling foil and closing at the top. Place on grill with medium heat about 10 to 15 minutes or until chocolate is melted and bananas are partially cooked. Open top of foil and gently push the ends of the banana to the middle (similar to the way you would a baked potato). Place in a dessert bowl or dish and add a big scoop of banana split ice cream (or a scoop each of chocolate, strawberry and chocolate). Top with whipped cream and a cherry. Now This is a dessert definitely fit for any avid barbecuer!

National BBQ Festival

Official dessert of the National BBQ Festival.

National BBQ Festival
Douglas • November

The best barbecue pitmasters in America will serve up their specialties for thousands who make their yearly pilgrimage to the annual National BBQ Festival held on the "Fall Forward Time Change" weekend each year. A total of more than $60,000 is paid out in cash and prizes. Competition events include the NBF Open, Backyard and Kid's Q, along with a big crowd favorite—the FNBCC People's Choice Competition. Sample BBQ from five competition teams and help choose the winner of the People's Choice Award with proceeds going to local charities. Other events include live entertainment, South Georgia's Gigantic Indoor Yard Sale, Holiday Bazaar and the Wiregrass Art Show and Sale.

800.385.0002
www.nationalbbqfestival.com

Nutty Nanner Pudding

1 box vanilla wafers, divided
3 to 4 bananas, sliced
2 boxes instant vanilla pudding
Milk as called for on pudding boxes
⅓ cup chopped Georgia peanuts or pecans
Whipped cream, optional

Layer ½ vanilla wafers over bottom of a glass baking dish. Layer sliced bananas over top of wafers. Prepare pudding as directed and pour over bananas. Crush remaining wafers into crumbs and sprinkle crumbs and chopped nuts over pudding. Chill to set. Serve with whipped cream, if desired.

Starr's Mill
Fayette County

Joan Soles • bigstockphoto.com

Strawberry Cheesecake Trifle

2 pints fresh strawberries, washed, capped and sliced
1 cup sugar, divided
2 (8-ounce) packages cream cheese, softened
3 tablespoons milk
1 (24-ounce) carton whipped topping
1 (10¾-ounce) loaf frozen pound cake, thawed and cut into ½-inch cubes
3 (1-ounce) squares semi-sweet chocolate, grated

Toss strawberries with ½ cup sugar; set aside. Beat cream cheese, milk, and remaining ½ cup sugar until smooth. Fold in whipped topping. Drizzle juice from strawberries over cake cubes. Place ½ cake cubes in 4-quart trifle dish or clear glass serving bowl. Top with ⅓ cream cheese mixture, ½ strawberries, and ½ chocolate; repeat layers. Top with remaining cream cheese mixture. Cover and refrigerate at least 4 hours before serving. Serves 14.

Pumpkin Cheesecake

1½ cups gingersnap cookie crumbs
¾ cup pecan pieces
1 cup plus 3 tablespoons brown sugar, divided
6 tablespoons unsalted butter, melted
3 (8-ounce) packages cream cheese, softened
1 cup brown sugar
1½ cups canned solid-pack pumpkin
½ cup heavy cream
⅓ cup maple syrup
1 tablespoon vanilla extract
¾ teaspoon ground cinnamon
½ teaspoon ground allspice
4 eggs

Preheat oven to 325°. Grease and flour a 9-inch springform pan. Using a fork, combine gingersnaps, pecan pieces, 3 tablespoons brown sugar and melted butter. Press onto bottom and 2 inches up sides of pan to form crust. With an electric mixer, beat cream cheese and brown sugar until light and fluffy. Stir in pumpkin. Mix in cream, maple syrup, vanilla, cinnamon and allspice. Beat in eggs, 1 at a time, mixing until smooth. Pour batter into prepared crust. Bake 90 minutes, or until center of cheesecake is set. Allow to cool in pan for 30 minutes, then refrigerate overnight. We suggest a bit of Vanilla Whipped topping as an extra flavorful touch.

Peach Pizza Perfection

½ cup butter, softened
¼ cup powdered sugar
1 cup sifted flour
1 cup sugar
2 tablespoons cornstarch
1 cup water
4 tablespoons cherry jello
8 to 10 large Georgia peaches
1 (8-ounce) container whipped topping

Cream butter; mix in powdered sugar. Add flour to form a soft dough. Pat on bottom and sides of a 12-inch pizza pan. Bake at 325° for 20 minutes; cool. Combine sugar, cornstarch and water; cook over low heat, stirring constantly, until thick and clear. Stir in gelatin; cool. Peel and slice peaches; arrange in a single layer over baked crust. Top with cooled glaze. Chill at least 1 hour or until ready to serve. Top with whipped topping before serving.

Index

A

B

C

Savannah Sidewalk • David S. Baker • shutterstock.com

Lillis Photography • istockphoto.com

W

Z

292 Recipes for 30 Varieties of Wild Game

The sportsman's outdoor experience doesn't end when the gun or the fishing gear has been put away. The challenge and reward of the quest are continued when the game is prepared into fabulous meals to be shared with friends and family.

Veteran hunter, fisherman, and chef Harold Webster delights sportsmen and those who cook game with seasonal recipes for venison, fish, fowl, and other delicacies from field and water. Fans of Webster's wild-game cookbooks and his popular newspaper column will recognize his trademark recipe clarity and his expert advice on handling, preparing, and serving game.

In addition to the recipes, Webster tells fascinating stories about the capturing, cleaning and cooking of the game. Stories like **Bow Season: Best Deer Hunt of the Year**, **Come Gather at Our Table**, **Stalking the Wild Fall Turkey**, and **Poochie was a Feist Dog** make this book an entertaining read as well as an essential resource for creating memorable meals from any hunter's bounty.

Game for All Seasons
$16.95 • 240 pp • 7 x 10
paperbound

Also available from Great American Publishers:

900 recipes make up this outstanding collection created with the everyday cook in mind. Each cookbook features 150 easy-to-prepare recipes using common ingredients that are easily found in your local grocery store (most will already be in your kitchen!).

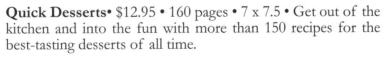

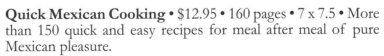

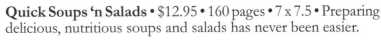

Quick Crockery Cooking • $12.95 • 160 pages • 7 x 7.5 • You'll be in and out of the kitchen fast with creative crockery recipes that are easy, economical and DELICIOUS.

Quick Desserts • $12.95 • 160 pages • 7 x 7.5 • Get out of the kitchen and into the fun with more than 150 recipes for the best-tasting desserts of all time.

Quick Hors d'oeuvres • $12.95 • 160 pages • 7 x 7.5 • Entertaining friends and family is a snap with quick and easy recipes for all-time favorite hors d'oeuvres and beverages.

Quick Lunches & Brunches • $12.95 • 160 pages • 7 x 7.5 • From Shrimp Scampi Kabobs to Caramel Muffins, impress friends and family with a delicious brunch made from 150 quick and easy recipes.

Quick Mexican Cooking • $12.95 • 160 pages • 7 x 7.5 • More than 150 quick and easy recipes for meal after meal of pure Mexican pleasure.

Quick Soups 'n Salads • $12.95 • 160 pages • 7 x 7.5 • Preparing delicious, nutritious soups and salads has never been easier.

State Hometown Cookbook Series
Collect Them All!

Each title in the **HOMETOWN COOKBOOK SERIES** contains FAVORITE recipes from Hometowns all over the state plus fun side-bars featuring food festivals throughout the state. This series is great for anyone who loves to cook, cookbook collectors, and armchair travelers. $16.95 each.

If not available locally, use the order form below, or call us toll-free **1.888.854.5954** or visit us on the web at **www.GreatAmericanPublishers.com**

Order Form
MAIL TO: **Great American Publishers • P. O. Box 1305 • Kosciusko, MS 39090**

❏ Check Enclosed

Charge to: ❏ Visa ❏ MC ❏ AmEx ❏ Disc

Card# _____

Exp Date _____ Signature _____

Name _____

Address _____

City _____ State _____ Zip _____

Phone_____

Email _____

Qty.	Title	Total
____	_____	_____
____	_____	_____
____	_____	_____
____	_____	_____
____	_____	_____
____	_____	_____
____	_____	_____

Subtotal _____

Postage ($3 1st book; $.50 each additional) _____

Total _____